HEAVY HITTER

- While still a few days away from graduating from high school, Junior was the Mariners' number-one draft pick and the first player chosen in the 1987 draft.

- When Ken Griffey, Sr., joined his son in Seattle in 1990, the two became the first father and son ever to play together in the same outfield.

- In 1997, Junior was named the American League's Most Valuable Player after hitting a career-high 56 home runs, the most by a left-handed batter since Roger Maris hit a record 61 in 1961.

Here's Ken Griffey, Jr., from his early years watching his father play professional baseball, to his starring role as a major home-run hitter. Read all about the outfielder who's truly in a league of his own.

KEN GRIFFEY, JR.:
A Biogra

D0770093

Books by Bill Gutman

Sports Illustrated: GREAT MOMENTS IN BASEBALL
Sports Illustrated: GREAT MOMENTS IN PRO FOOTBALL
BASEBALL SUPER TEAMS
BO JACKSON: A BIOGRAPHY
FOOTBALL SUPER TEAMS
GRANT HILL: A BIOGRAPHY
GREAT QUARTERBACKS OF THE NFL
GREAT SPORTS UPSETS
GREAT SPORTS UPSETS 2
KEN GRIFFEY, JR.: A BIOGRAPHY
MICHAEL JORDAN: A BIOGRAPHY
NBA HIGH-FLYERS
PRO SPORTS CHAMPIONS
SHAQUILLE O'NEAL: A BIOGRAPHY
TIGER WOODS: A BIOGRAPHY

Available from ARCHWAY Paperbacks

KEN GRIFFEY JR.

A Biography

BILL GUTMAN

AN ARCHWAY PAPERBACK
Published by POCKET BOOKS
New York London Toronto Sydney Tokyo Singapore

AN ARCHWAY PAPERBACK *Original*

An Archway Paperback published by
POCKET BOOKS, a division of Simon & Schuster Inc.
1230 Avenue of the Americas, New York, NY 10020

ISBN: 0-671-02065-X

First Archway Paperback printing May 1998

10 9 8 7 6 5 4 3 2 1

AN ARCHWAY PAPERBACK and colophon are
registered trademarks of Simon & Schuster Inc.

Cover photo by Focus on Sports

Printed in the U.S.A.

IL: 7

For Cathy

Introduction

He is simply called *Junior*. No fancy nicknames to describe his enormous talent and widespread charisma. *Junior*. That says it all. It tells sports fans everywhere that we're talking about Ken Griffey, Jr., widely considered the best all-around player in the major leagues today.

His credentials for that lofty claim are impeccable. Already a nine-year veteran of the big league wars by the end of 1997, Junior was still just twenty-seven years old and coming off the greatest season of his career. Not only did he lead the major leagues with 147 runs batted in, but he also slammed 56 home runs, the most by a left-handed batter since Roger Maris hit a record 61 in 1961. After the season he was named the American League's Most Valuable Player and added an eighth straight Gold Glove for his defensive prowess in the outfield.

Yet he does it all so effortlessly that he has also been called, simply, The Natural. Whether it's his fluid left-handed swing or a circus catch in the outfield, Ken Griffey, Jr., always looks as if he was born to play baseball. And in a real sense, he was. His father, Ken Griffey, Sr., was an outstanding player for several teams during a very solid nineteen-year career.

In fact, the senior Griffey was part of the great Cincinnati Reds "Big Red Machine" clubs during the 1970s, at the same time his eldest son was getting his introduction to the game. So Junior grew up around the likes of Pete Rose, Johnny Bench, Joe Morgan, Dave Concepcion, and the rest of the players on those great teams. Quite an introduction to big league life.

Junior's own talent was in evidence early. He was the number one draft choice of the Mariners in 1987 when he was just seventeen years old, and three years later made family history when he and his father played in the same big league outfield together. It was a great way for Senior to go out and a better way for Junior to come in. The torch was passed, and now there has been a Griffey in the major leagues since 1973.

In the mid-1990s, the Seattle Mariners have become one of baseball's most exciting and interesting teams. Surrounded by a number of outstanding hitters, Junior continues to improve and put huge numbers on the board. His number one priority has never been his own statistics, but rather helping his team win a world championship. Baseball fans just love watching him play—enjoying his boyish enthusiasm, his broad smile, and his enormous skills. They realize they are watching a living legend, a player who will someday be enshrined in the Baseball Hall of Fame at Cooperstown, New York.

But before that happens, Ken Griffey, Jr., will continue to play with the brand of style and exuberance that has made him the most popular player in the game, a player who continues to bring new fans out to ballparks all around the league. There is just one *Junior*, and this is his story.

Chapter 1

Born into a
Baseball Life

The wheels that would drive Ken Griffey, Jr.'s baseball career began turning long before he was born. In fact, the seeds may have been sown as far back as 1920. That was the year Stanley Frank Musial was born in Donora, Pennsylvania. To baseball fans, Musial became known as "Stan the Man" and was one of the greatest players ever to don a pair of spikes.

But what does Stan Musial have to do with Ken Griffey, Jr.? Simple. It's the Donora connection. That was the Pennsylvania town where Ken Griffey, Sr., was born in 1950. And as he grew up during the 1950s, Musial was in his prime with the St. Louis Cardinals, one of baseball's greatest stars.

Musial's presence alone made most kids in Donora want to play baseball. Ken, Sr., was no exception. And he had yet another connection. His father, Buddy Griffey, knew Stan the Man. They had been teammates at Donora High School, where Buddy was a left-handed-throwing third baseman. The elder Griffey was also a football star at Donora. So the athletic genes in the family ran deep.

But that didn't always make life easy for Ken, Sr. Buddy Griffey left the family when Ken, Sr., was just two. He was raised in his early years by his mother, Ruth, who had five other children she supported by working odd jobs and sometimes having to accept welfare checks. Buddy Griffey came back into his family's life some seven years later. When he returned and knocked at the door, Ken answered it and didn't even recognize his father. The two never regained the closeness that a father and son should have. And that is undoubtedly one reason why Ken, Sr., made it a point to always remain close to *his* sons.

Ken, Sr., was into sports his entire young life. By the time he reached Donora High, he was not only a baseball star, but excelled at track and football as well. Those who remember say baseball was probably Ken's weakest sport of the three, but he still had great natural ability. A scout for the Cincinnati Reds saw that ability and thought Ken might someday develop into a major leaguer. In 1969, the Reds took a chance, but not a major one. They picked Ken Griffey, Sr., on the twenty-ninth round of the 1969 draft.

A low pick doesn't even rate a signing bonus, but Ken, Sr., still saw it as an opportunity. Though just nineteen years old, Ken was already married, and his wife, Alberta, was expecting their first child. Ken spent the remainder of the 1969 season in the low minors. Then, on November 21 of that year, George Kenneth Griffey, Jr., was born. Like his father, Ken, Jr., was also born in Donora, Pennsylvania, keeping alive the tradition that went back to the great Stan Musial. And nearly two years later, a second son, Craig, was also born there.

Ken, Sr., would spend four years in the minors. With the low pay of the minor leaguer, things weren't easy for the young family. But in other ways it was a good time, because the family stayed together, giving them a chance to forge a real closeness.

"The days in the minor leagues were the best times," Ken, Sr., remembers, "because that's when I developed a closeness with [my sons]. I was always with them. I had them all the time."

Though he spent a great deal of time with his family, Ken, Sr., also worked hard to develop his talent for the game. By 1973 he was called up with the Reds for the first time, playing in 25 games and hitting .384. He was a solid, five-foot-eleven 190-pounder with outstanding speed, and it was becoming apparent quickly that the senior Griffey had big league potential.

A year later, in 1974, he played in 88 games for the Reds and fell off to .251, but a year later he made the club and was more or less a regular. Playing in 132 games, Griffey hit .305, scored 95 runs, and had 4 homers and 46 RBIs. But there was more to the story than that. Ken, Sr., was now a member of the best team in baseball. The 1975

Reds won 108 regular season games and would win the World Series in a memorable battle with the Boston Red Sox.

The starting lineup read like an All-Star team, with Tony Perez at first, Joe Morgan at second, Dave Concepcion at short, and Pete Rose at third. In the outfield, right fielder Griffey was joined by George Foster in left and Cesar Geronimo in center. The group was collectively tabbed the Big Red Machine for their ability to hit and score runs. And this was the baseball atmosphere in which Ken, Jr., grew up.

It wasn't long before the slim youngster began showing signs of following in his father's footsteps. He knew the game very well from an early age. Following the 1975 season, Ken, Sr., decided to play winter ball in Puerto Rico. The family went along with him. Ken, Jr., was just six years old then. In one game, Ken, Sr., struck out early in the game. Trying to encourage his father, Junior said, "That pitcher's got nothing."

The next time Senior came up, he promptly struck out again. When he returned to the dugout he again heard the voice of his young son. This time Junior took another approach.

"Dad, *you* got nothing!" he shouted.

The next year, 1976, the Big Red Machine were World Champs again, this time sweeping the New York Yankees in four straight games. And Ken Griffey, Sr., seemed on the brink of becoming a real star. He batted a career best .336 in 148 games, adding six homers, nine triples, and 74 RBIs. He also scored 111 runs and stole 34 bases.

And at that time, the most heralded team in baseball was really like a big family. Despite so many star players, the team always came first and the players were all good friends. That meant families often got together. The players often brought their sons into the locker room and onto the field. All the young boys really got themselves a baseball education.

Spending so much time at Riverfront Stadium gave Junior the chance not only to meet many great players, but to frolic with their young sons as well. He would play catch at various times with Pete Rose, Jr., Eduardo and Victor Perez, Lee May, Jr., and Brian McRae. No one knew it at the time, but it would be Ken, Jr., who would far outshine the rest of them when it came to overall talent. But as a group of kids, they were often called the "Little Red Machine."

"They were wild, and you had to keep after them," said Tony Perez, the team's slugging first baseman. "But they were all good kids."

So life was good for Ken, Jr., and the rest of the family. Ken, Sr., hit over .300 in three of the next five seasons, though injuries limited his playing time on two occasions. As a team, the Reds were beginning to age and, while still a winning ball club, didn't reach the World Series again. During that time, young Ken was getting taller and playing all the baseball he could.

He played organized ball for the first time in the summer of 1980. It was for a summer recreation league team, the A&A Janitorial Service. He was just ten years old, but because he was already so good he was often heckled by parents of players on the opposing team. They thought he was older than the other kids and didn't want him out there. Alberta Griffey was forced to bring Junior's birth certificate to every game because someone was always questioning his age.

By then he was the team's best hitter and best pitcher, and could play every position on the field. His mother didn't want to see him hold back and would encourage him to "strike out the next three batters. Then we'll really hear them."

Sure enough, Junior would strike out the side and the fans would boo him some more. They just couldn't accept the fact that he was so much better than their sons. But that was just the beginning. Parents, opposing players, and other fans would soon have to get used to the fact that Ken Griffey, Jr., was better than his own teammates and the opposing players. It wasn't long before his talent was so great that there were predictions he would soon be following in the footsteps of his father.

Chapter 2

Nothing Stays the Same

The same summer that Junior was playing for A&A Janitorial, Ken, Sr., was having another fine year for the Reds. At midseason he was chosen to play in the 1980 All-Star Game at Dodger Stadium in Los Angeles. Up to that time, Ken, Jr., sort of took his father's baseball career for granted. It had always been part of his life, and he enjoyed playing ball with kids his age rather than following the big leaguers. But looking back, he says the All-Star Game that year was his most vivid memory from the early years.

"That's the one time Dad impressed me [as a ballplayer]," Junior said. "He hit a home run and was named the Most Valuable Player of the game. But mostly it didn't matter what he did on the field. He was just Dad."

Ken, Sr., had a great game. Besides the homer, he had another base hit as the National League won, 4–2. Junior was about to start playing Little League ball and his father was in his prime as a top player in the National League. But nothing stays the same. The following year, 1981, the big league season was shortened by a players' strike. While the Reds had the best overall record in the National League, they didn't make the playoffs because of the peculiarities of the split season, broken in two by the strike.

Though Ken, Sr., hit a solid .311 that year, it was apparent that the Reds were no longer the Big Red Machine. They had won more with pitching than slugging and team officials felt it was time to rebuild. Ken was just thirty-one years old with plenty of good baseball left in him. But he was one of the players the team decided to move. In the off-season he was traded to the New York Yankees.

While Ken, Sr., had high hopes going to the Yankees, there was one immediate change. It was decided that the rest of the Griffey family would remain in their home in Cincinnati. From that point on, Ken didn't see as much of his family during the baseball season. And that meant he also didn't see Junior's amazing development as a ballplayer. At least not close up.

The younger Griffey continued to grow and improve. He was outstanding at every level of play. While his father had more of a strong, stocky build, Junior began to look as if he would be long and lanky. He was quickly becoming an outstanding, all-around athlete, smooth as silk at everything he did. And if there was a problem, he could always contact his dad by phone.

"If I needed to talk to him, I would call him after the game," Junior said. "If I did something wrong [on the field] Dad would sometimes fly me to New York and tell me what I should have done. Then he would send me home the next day, and I'd play baseball."

Not a bad deal, getting flown to New York to work with a personal coach who also happened to be your father. Maybe it was a fringe benefit, but it was Junior's great talent that was already attracting attention. Big league scouts began noticing him when he was just fourteen years old. He was already tabbed a future professional ballplayer. And that would come a lot sooner than anyone could have predicted.

Junior entered Moeller High School in Cincinnati as a freshman in the fall of 1983. Moeller had a national reputation as a football power, a school that sent many athletes on to top-flight college football programs. Most good athletes who went to Moeller wound up playing football. Junior Griffey was no exception. Everyone knew he was a lock for the baseball team as a freshman, but he also made the football team as a speedy tailback.

In his first three years at Moeller, Ken, Jr., starred in both sports. He was a hard-hitting outfielder on the baseball team, and a slashing tailback and speedy wide receiver on the football squad. The irony was that Ken, Sr., often saw his son play football, since the gridiron season took place after baseball ended. He never saw him play baseball in the spring because he himself was still playing.

"Because I hadn't really seen his baseball development for myself, I began to think he might have a future in football," the elder Griffey said.

But those who saw him play baseball continually knew how good he was. When he was sixteen and at Moeller, Junior also wanted to play summer baseball in the Connie Mack League. That's an amateur league with teams throughout the country. Though most of the Connie Mack League players were older, Alberta Griffey felt her son was ready to join them. But Ken, Sr., balked at the suggestion. He was away again and, because he hadn't seen his son play much, thought Junior might be overmatched by the older boys in the league.

It took Mrs. Griffey several months to convince Ken, Sr., that their son was ready. When he was finally allowed to join, all Junior did was lead his team to the Connie Mack World Series, where he hit three home runs: one to left, one to center, and the other to right field. He already had great power.

Perhaps because he was away from home so much, Ken, Sr., always worried about his son. When Junior's Connie Mack team, the Midland Cardinals, were on the road the senior Griffey always left orders for Junior to check in with him. He knew all the players on the team were older than his son and didn't want anyone having a bad influence on the sixteen-year-old.

One night, Junior knocked on Coach Joe Hayden's door and asked to use the phone to check in with his father. When he hung up, he asked the coach if he could spend the night in Hayden's room. The reason was Ken, Sr.

"My dad wants to call later to make sure I'm not out misbehaving," Junior said.

The coach agreed and, sure enough, at 3 A.M. the phone rang. It was Ken, Sr., just making sure everything was all right. But while Ken, Sr., was a disciplinarian who wanted to make sure his boys earned everything they got, he was also very generous with them.

"Have I spoiled Kenny and Craig?" Ken, Sr., once asked, then answered his own question without a pause. "Hell, yeah, I spoiled them. I wanted them to have what I couldn't."

It was a tough balancing act, but so far it seemed to be working.

In his junior baseball season of 1986, Ken was named Player of the Year in the conference, though he was not yet seventeen years old. As good as he was, however, there was still one thing that bothered Junior on the baseball field—that was those rare occasions when his father was in the stands. His coach at Moeller, Mike Cameron, remembered what would happen.

"A hundred scouts could be in the stands and it wouldn't make a difference to Junior," Cameron said. "Only when his father was there would Kenny pressure himself."

Junior admitted that for a time he always found himself trying too hard when his father was around.

"When he was there was the only time I thought I had to impress somebody," he explained. "But he would always tell me he was the one guy I *didn't* have to impress."

It took a while for those words of wisdom to sink in. As hard as it was to believe, the younger Griffey hadn't gotten a single hit when his father was at a game from 1982 to 1987. That might have simply been the pressure of trying to follow in the footsteps of a famous father. Everyone in Cincinnati remembered how good Ken Griffey, Sr., had been with the Big Red Machine.

Griffey, Sr., had moved on since that time. He was with the Yankees from 1982 through the beginning of the 1986 season. It wasn't like the great days in Cincinnati. The Yanks used him as a platoon player, though he usually got more than 400 at-bats. Yet he hit .300 only once, a .306 mark in 1983. Then, after playing 59 games for the Yanks in 1986, he was traded to the Atlanta Braves. He finished the year with the Braves and had a combined .306 batting average for both teams. He also slammed a career-best 21 home runs that year. At age thirty-six, he felt he could still play. How much longer, however, he didn't know.

That same year, his son made a major decision. In the fall of 1986, a month before the big league season ended, Junior was beginning his senior year at Moeller. He decided on his own not to play football that year. He was slated to be a starter and was expected to be one of the stars of the team. But he knew baseball was his best sport and that the big league scouts would be flocking to see him in the spring. He felt he couldn't jeopardize that by risking a serious injury playing football.

"It was his [Ken, Jr.'s] decision and his alone," his father said. "I wanted to see him play football, but he had all these baseball scouts watching him, and all he talked about was playing baseball."

By this time, Ken, Jr., stood six feet three inches tall and weighed a solid 195 pounds. Like his father, he batted from the left side of the plate and also threw left-handed. But while his father had a short, compact batting stroke, Junior had a full, smooth swing capable of generating great power. And he showed his full repertoire of skills his entire senior season, easily becoming Player of the Year in the conference for the second time. Junior was just seventeen years old, but was about to follow in his father's footsteps, becoming the second Griffey to be playing professional baseball.

Chapter 3

Best in the Nation

The annual major league draft was held on June 2, 1987. The first pick that year belonged to the Seattle Mariners of the American League's Western Division. The Mariners were an expansion team in 1977 and, like most new teams, had problems developing a winner. The team was 64–98 its first season, and in its tenth season of 1986 finished at 67–95. Not much of a change.

In fact, the Mariners never had a winning season and were losers of more than 100 games on three occasions. Three other times the team lost more than 90 games in a season. They had also gone through seven managers during those ten years. So the Mariners remained a team in flux and there were already questions whether they would remain in Seattle, where attendance wasn't very good. What the team needed was a real superstar, a franchise player around which to build.

With all this in mind, the Seattle brain trust went out and made seventeen-year-old Ken Griffey, Jr., their number one draft pick and the first player chosen in the 1987 draft. That was quite a vote of confidence for a youngster who was still a few days away from graduating from high school. And it also put the pressure on. While no one expected Junior to make it to the major leagues immediately, there was still a great deal of pressure to succeed, even if he didn't feel it at the time.

"My son considers himself a winner," Ken, Sr., said. "He feels that one day he can help turn the franchise around."

A few days after graduating from Moeller High, Junior signed with the Mariners for a bonus of about $160,000. That was $160,000 more than his father had gotten as a twenty-ninth draft choice. But times had changed. Everything was on the fast track. As soon as Junior signed, he was sent to the Mariners' Class A team in Bellingham, Washington, a town some ninety miles north of Seattle and just twenty miles from the Canadian border.

Bellingham was in the Northwest League, which played a short season. It gave teenagers and first-time pros like Junior a chance to get a feel for the professional game—from the travel, to being away from home, to playing nearly every day. It wasn't always an easy adjustment. But at seventeen, Ken, Jr., was a young man in a hurry. He used to tell his new teammates that his stay in the minors would be a short one.

"I'll be here one week, then move to San Bernardino [Class A, full season], then Double-A the week after that. I gotta be in the Show [the Major Leagues] when I'm eighteen, because I'll have no money left."

Later, he would admit it was only his youth talking. "That was when I was young and dumb," he would say with a wink.

But it wouldn't take long for Junior to show everyone he was the real thing on the field. Off the field, however, there were other adjustments that had to be made. And some of these weren't easy for him at all. For openers, he was away from home for the first time and Bellingham was very different from Pennsylvania or Cincinnati in a number of ways, not the least of which was that there were very few black people there.

"Things are a little different here," Junior said. "It will take some getting used to for me. But I have to mature. That's why I'm here."

It didn't help when two teenage boys began calling him "nigger," among other things. Later, Junior would say that one of them threatened to come after him with a gun. It wasn't an easy thing for a seventeen-year-old to deal with, especially one who had to concentrate on playing baseball every day.

So at the beginning of the shortened season, Junior had his ups and downs. His first hit came against the Everett team on June 17. Junior picked out a fastball and drove it deep into the right field seats for a home run! You can't start a professional career any better than that. And it happened a little over two weeks after he had graduated from high school. During the remainder of that first week he hit three homers, drove home eight runs, and swiped four bases. He looked like a superstar in the making and was rewarded by being named Northwest League Player of the Week.

But there were setbacks as well. He was picked off first base on two occasions those first weeks because of a lack of concentration. He almost seemed to be daydreaming.

"He's got to learn to stay ahead mentally," said Billingham's manager, Rick Sweet. "You can't be a spectator when you're out there playing the game."

Then there were the long bus rides. Besides having to deal with racial slurs, Junior had to get used to bus rides up to ten hours long. The bus dated back to 1958 and didn't even have a bathroom.

"Conditions were a whole lot worse than I ever imagined," Junior would say later.

Those conditions and the pressures he was under led to an old-fashioned case of homesickness. Junior missed his family and friends, running up huge phone bills back to Cincinnati. There were times when he thought he wasn't ready for this and almost packed up and headed home. His mother and girlfriend encouraged him to stick it out.

Then he went into a batting slump that saw his average fall to .230, a far cry from what is expected of a number one draft choice. Finally his mother decided to fly from Cincinnati to Washington to see her son in person.

"When I can't hit, that's when I want to quit," Junior told her.

Alberta Griffey also learned that Junior had been benched for one game for violating the team curfew. That kind of behavior she wouldn't tolerate.

"The night before I left I gave it to him up one side and down the other," she remembered. "After that, he didn't call me for four days."

But the message got through. There was another brief setback when Junior crashed into the center field wall trying to make a catch on July 4. He injured his shoulder and had to sit out a week. But when he returned on July 12, he suddenly looked like the ballplayer the Mariners had drafted number one. For the next month he simply caught fire and played his heart out.

From July 12 through August 13, Ken, Jr., had a .453 batting average with seven homers and 16 RBIs. Almost overnight, it seemed, he had become the most exciting player in the league. Besides his great hitting, he was playing an outstanding center field, making catches all over the place and exhibiting a powerful throwing arm. When the season ended, he had achieved his initial goal. He had definitely established himself as a bona fide prospect and future star.

In 54 games, Ken, Jr., batted a solid .313, sixth best mark in the league. Among his 57 hits were nine doubles, one triple, 14 home runs, and 40 runs batted in. He also used his speed to steal 13 bases. He finished as the team leader in homers, RBIs, and steals, and was named to the all-league team. In addition, *Baseball America* magazine named him the top major league prospect in the Northwest League. It seemed as if he was on his way.

Before returning home to Cincinnati, the Mariners sent Junior to spend some time in the Arizona Instructional League. There he worked repetitively on the fundamentals of the game with a number of coaches who specialized in tutoring very young players. Finally, that fall, Junior returned home to Cincinnai and to what would be the biggest and most dangerous crisis of his young life.

When he finally came home he had already been through a very difficult year, one in which he had to make several major adjustments. He had begun the year as a high school senior, enjoying his final year with many of the friends he had known since he was a young kid. In addition, he was a star athlete and popular figure at Moeller. For him, it was a totally relaxed atmosphere. Then, days before his graduation, he learned he was major league baseball's number one draft choice, the top prospect in the entire nation. That's pressure right there.

Then he signed a contract that brought him a $160,000 bonus. Suddenly he had a pile of his own money. But before he could enjoy that, he was off to Bellingham, Washington, a strange place where he had to meet new teammates, had to deal with tough coaches, and had to face some unfamiliar racial slurs. But he made the adjustments. Then he was shipped to Arizona, where he had to adjust all over again. For a seventeen-year-old away from home for the first time, the year couldn't have been easy.

Needless to say, Junior came home that fall a somewhat different person than the one who had left a year earlier. He was probably looking for things to be just the same as they were before. But suddenly he found a lot of tension between his father and himself, something that had never really existed before.

"It seemed like everyone was yelling at me in baseball," Junior would say later. "Then I came home and everyone was yelling at me there."

Because Junior was now earning his own money, his father felt that he should begin paying his way around the house. It was probably a matter of a father wanting his son to learn about responsibility and not become a spoiled young athlete. But both were sensitive and tempers soon flared. It came to a head in January 1988.

"Dad wanted me to pay rent or get my own place," Ken, Jr., recalled. "I was confused. I got depressed and angry. Because I was hurting, I wanted to cause some hurt for others. And I didn't want to live."

One day Junior was with his girlfriend when he suddenly opened a bottle of aspirin and swallowed all the pills. His girlfriend and her brother tried to stop him but couldn't. He then got in his car, but before he could drive off he got sick and threw up. His girlfriend's mother then drove him quickly to a nearby hospital. There, doctors pumped his stomach and put him in intensive care.

Ken, Sr., said he was both frightened and angry

when he found out what his son had done. He rushed to the hospital, but as soon as he saw Junior the two got into yet another argument.

"I just ripped the IV out of my arm," Junior said, "and that stopped him from yelling."

Finally, both father and son realized they had some major problems to resolve, and they did it through long, heart-to-heart talks. They talked about everything that was bothering them, as well as all the good times they'd had. They continued talking right up until both left for spring training, and they haven't stopped talking to each other since. It was the one and only time they had clashed that way, but it could have resulted in a real tragedy. Fortunately, both realized they had to talk about their problems, not hold them in and allow them to build.

Later, Junior admitted that he had thought about killing himself a couple of times. "The aspirin thing was the only time I acted," he said. "It was such a dumb thing."

At the time of the incident, no one outside the immediate family and the few others involved knew about it. Both father and son left for spring training in March 1988 right on schedule. It wasn't until 1992 that Junior decided to talk publicly about the incident for the first time. He originally recounted what had happened during an interview with the *Seattle Times*, saying that he was going public with the story in the hope it might dissuade others from seeing suicide as a solution to their problems.

The story shocked many people who already

knew Junior as a big league superstar. But it pointed out the pressures on teenagers who are thrust into the world of professional athletics. And it also may have pointed out the special difficulties that can be encountered by a son trying to follow in the footsteps of a famous father. Fortunately, both Griffeys, Junior and Senior, were able to come to grips with their problems and were willing to work very hard at solving them. Stories like this don't always have happy endings.

But in the spring of 1988 it was back to baseball. Ken, Sr., at age thirty-eight, began the season with the Atlanta Braves. He would, however, be traded once more. Halfway through the season he was shipped back to his first team, the Cincinnati Reds. In effect, Ken, Sr., had come home. Perhaps he felt then that it would be nice to finish his career in the place where it had started. Neither Griffey knew it then, but a more interesting finish for Ken, Sr., would still lie ahead.

As for Junior, the Mariners sent him to San Bernardino, a Class-A team in the California league and a step up from Bellingham. Before he left for spring training, he got some advice from Mike Cameron, his former coach at Moeller High.

Said Cameron, "Before he went down I told him, 'Kenny, you've got to get serious. This is a great opportunity for you to make a nice living.' He looked like he was listening hard. Then he said, 'I can't wait to get there. I'm going to get in a pillow fight.'"

Junior's happy-go-lucky attitude was a sign of his

youth. It was also beginning to look as if he would be making a typical "trip" through the minors. Many clubs want their young prospects to take it step by step. First Class-A, then Double-A, and finally, Triple-A. At each level, the caliber of play is a little bit better. If a prospect succeeds at all levels, then he is given a real shot to make the big club, the Show. What no one in the Mariners family knew then was the amazing progress young Ken Griffey, Jr., was about to make.

From day one, Junior was the everyday center fielder for the San Bernardino Spirit and he looked as if he was born to play there. He was hitting well and covering the outfield like a blanket. Then, early in the season, the Braves had a game with the Dodgers in Los Angeles. After the game, Ken, Sr., rented a car for the eighty-mile drive down the coast to see his son play.

It was a start of opposites for the Griffeys. The Braves had lost their first 10 games and Ken, Sr., was struggling with an .091 average. By contrast, San Bernardino was 7–0 and Junior was hitting over .500 early in the season. When the kids at the Spirit game heard who was there, they mobbed Ken, Sr., for autographs. Then he settled down to watch his son play professional ball for only the second time. The one other game he had seen the year before, Junior only pinch-hit and struck out.

"There are so many things I don't know because I haven't seen him," Ken, Sr., said.

When Junior came up in the bottom of the first inning, the public address announcer cried out to the crowd of nearly twenty-five hundred fans, "YES, INDEEDY, BOYS AND GIRLS. WHAT TIME IS IT?"

Without a pause, the fans answered in unison, "IT'S GRIFFEY TIME!"

It didn't take his father long to see who the big hero was in San Bernardino. His first time up Junior showed his versatility. He was already one of the top sluggers in the league, but this time he laid a perfect bunt down the third base line and beat it out without drawing a throw.

"I was determined to get at least one hit [in front of Dad], even if he gets on me about [bunting]," Junior said.

Sure enough, his father later teased him about being a "Judy," which stands for Punch and Judy hitter, an expression reserved for players with virtually no power at the plate.

Then, in the third inning, Junior hit into a fielder's choice. But when he came up in the fifth there were runners on first and third. Using a bat that his father had brought for him, he smacked an infield single to the right side, driving home a run. In the sixth inning, he showed his father and everyone else still another side to his game.

Playing in center as always, he raced quickly into left center to cut off a ball that was bouncing toward the fence. His great speed and quick throw held the runner to a single. Later in the inning, with a runner on third, he caught a long fly ball, and while he didn't really have a chance to nail the tagging runner, he still fired a bullet to home plate.

"I'd like to borrow some of that," Ken, Sr., said, referring to his son's throwing arm.

Finally, it was the bottom of the eighth and Junior came up once again. By this time San Bernardino had a 9–5 lead. The bases were empty, so Junior would have a chance to really swing away. He worked the count full at 3-2, then got a pitch he liked. He took that long, smooth swing and hit a rocket high and deep toward left. The ball cleared the fence and a clump of eucalyptus trees behind it, landing more than 400 feet from home plate.

Junior circled the bases with a big smile on his face. When he crossed the plate he pointed a teasing finger toward his father in the press box, as if to say, "Top that."

After taking Junior and a handful of his teammates out to dinner, Ken, Sr., drove back to Los Angeles. From there, he quickly phoned his wife to give her a scouting report on their son.

"Bertie," he said, "I saw something from him in all five categories today [hitting, hitting for power, running, throwing, and fielding]. It doesn't make sense for someone to have that much talent."

But it was quickly becoming apparent that Junior, indeed, had the talent. He was just eighteen years old and beginning to look more and more like a big leaguer in waiting. His father, with his own career winding down, now had something else to look forward to. Asked what he felt while watching his son play, Ken, Sr., answered quickly.

"Enjoyment," he said. "That's what I feel watching him. Enjoyment."

Chapter 4

The Youngest Player in the Majors

By the time San Bernardino had played just 24 games, Junior was burning up the league. He was the leader in all three triple-crown categories, sporting a .520 batting average with four homers and 11 RBIs. He continued to play top-flight baseball into early June. Then, once more, his all-out effort in the outfield caused an injury. On June 9, he tried to make a diving catch after a long run and injured his back. He would go on the disabled list for nearly five weeks.

In 58 games prior to his injury, Junior was hitting .338 with 13 doubles, three triples, 11 home runs, and 42 RBIs. He also stole 32 bases. When he went on the disabled list he was leading the league in home runs, in total bases with 126, and in steals. And he was second in hitting, as well. The Mariners were so impressed that when he was ready to play again in August, they promoted him to their Double-A team in Vermont of the Eastern League.

It was already late in the season when he reached Vermont. Because his back was still sore, he was used mainly as a designated hitter for the final 17 games of the regular season. Though he hit just .279 with two homers and 10 RBIs, he was obviously not 100 percent. He saved that for the Eastern League playoffs.

All he did in the playoffs was hit .444, getting eight hits in 18 at-bats and driving home a club-high seven runs in the series against Pittsfield. When the season ended he learned that *Baseball America* had once again picked him as the top major league prospect in the California League. And he had missed five weeks due to injury. Though not yet nineteen years old, his future now seemed limitless.

The off-season was one of mixed feelings for the Griffeys. The 1988 season hadn't been a good one for Ken, Sr. He had hit just .249 as a part-timer with the Braves, appearing in just 69 games. Then, in the latter part of the season, the Braves released him. He thought it might be the end of the line, but he was then signed by his first team, the Cincinnati Reds. He finished the year by playing in parts of 25 games with Cincy, hitting .280, giving him an overall average of .255, his lowest mark since becoming a regular.

Though he would be going to training camp with the Reds, Ken, Sr., didn't know what to expect. Junior, on the other hand, had been invited to the Mariners' camp as a nonroster player. That meant he was still officially a minor leaguer and chances of his sticking with the big club were slim. Yet anyone at spring training had a chance to make it. And that brought up an interesting possibility.

Throughout the long history of baseball, no father and son had ever played in the major leagues at the same time. But if Ken, Sr., could stick with the Reds at age thirty-nine, and Junior could make it with the Mariners at age nineteen, they would become a family first, a baseball curiosity. That possibility probably motivated both of them when spring training rolled around, though up to this point Ken, Sr., never thought it would happen.

"It took me four-and-a-half years to make the big leagues," the senior Griffey said. "When Junior signed, I thought it would take that long for him. I thought I would be coaching or be a hitting instructor by then."

Because the senior Griffey had been such a solid ballplayer for so many years, the Reds knew they could use him as a part-time outfielder and pinch hitter. Always in good physical condition, Ken, Sr., showed he could still play by hitting .333 in his first 21 spring at-bats. So he would be gearing up for his seventeenth season in the majors. But what about Junior?

The prevalent opinion was that he needed a season of Triple-A ball just to give him another taste of the professional game at the highest level of the minors. The Mariners' top farm club was in

Calgary in the Pacific Coast League, and that was where most observers figured Junior would land. But at the same time, Seattle manager Jim Lefebvre wanted to give him a real shot in the spring.

"I want to take a good look at him," Lefebvre said. "Then we'll see how it goes."

So Junior was out in center nearly every day during the preseason games. His manager, the coaches, and most of his teammates waited for the inexperience to show, waited to see how he would handle a slump, waited for him to play himself out of the lineup. It never happened.

From day one, Ken, Jr., showed everyone that he could indeed handle major league pitching. In addition, he was the best outfielder in camp and he didn't seem awestruck going up against big league veterans who had been around for years. He had one of the best spring trainings for a rookie that anyone could remember. When reporters asked him why he seemed to take things so calmly, he answered, "Man, this is my twelfth spring training camp. That's ten with my dad and two on my own."

Maybe all those years he hung around the great Cincinnati teams when he was a kid made things easier. He had seen the routine so many times before and was ready. What he did was certainly eye-opening.

Junior played in 26 preseason games and hit a whopping .359, with two homers and 21 RBIs. He set Mariner records for preseason games with 33 hits and his 21 ribbys. In addition, he had a 15-game hitting streak during the spring and wasn't overmatched against any pitcher he faced. He also played great defense and ran the bases like a seasoned veteran. When it came time to bring the major league roster down to twenty-five players, the Mariners really didn't have a choice. At age nineteen, Ken Griffey, Jr., had made the team.

About a week before the season Junior was called to Manager Lefebvre's office. He thought he was going to be told that he'd be starting the season in Calgary. Instead, he got the surprise of his young life.

"Congratulations," the manager told him. "You're my starting center fielder."

Junior's mouth dropped open in shock. It was like a dream come true. He really didn't know what to say.

"When he said that, my heart started ticking again," Junior said later. "Those were probably the best words I've ever heard."

Once the news got out, there were all kinds of stories about the Griffeys being the first father and son to play in the majors at the same time. In fact, some reporters asked Manager Lefebvre if that was the main reason he decided to open the season with Junior in center.

"Sure, it makes a good story," Lefebvre snapped. "But I didn't bring [Junior] onto this ball club because he's a good story. He's earned a spot here. He outplayed a lot of people for that spot."

So when the 1989 season opened, nineteen-year-old Ken Griffey, Jr., trotted out to center field for the Mariners. He was wearing number 24, the number worn by the player he most admired, speedy Rickey Henderson. Not only was he the youngest player in the majors, but he and his father made history as the first father-son duo to play in the big league at the same time. It made them both proud. But Junior also acknowledged that being the son of a successful player wasn't the easiest way to forge your own identity.

"It's harder being a son when your father is a baseball player," Junior said. "People will say, 'Your dad hit .300 lifetime, so you have to hit .310 to be better.' They put you in a category with your father, and that's not fair because you are two different people."

And two different ballplayers. Junior was taller and with a thinner build. Yet he was the more powerful hitter, with that picture-perfect swing. His father had been a very solid ballplayer, a star for several seasons. Yet he hadn't really made that final jump to the so-called superstar level. In the eyes of everyone who saw him, Junior had future superstar written all over him. But no matter what happened, both knew there would always be comparisons. They would have to live with it.

From the beginning, Junior looked as if he would continue the pace he set in the spring. The Mariners opened the season visiting the A's at Oakland. They were facing one of the league's best pitchers in right-hander Dave Stewart. In Junior's first-ever big league at-bat he picked out a Stewart pitch and slammed a double. A week later, in his very first at-bat before the home fans in the King-dome, he blasted his first big league homer, an opposite-field shot off Eric King of the White Sox.

Then, between April 23 and 27, he set a new Mariners record by banging out eight consecutive hits and reaching base 11 straight times. For his efforts he was named American League Player of the Week. He was taking the league by storm. Former major leaguer Gene Clines, the Mariners' hitting coach, was one of many who were totally impressed by Junior's amazing play.

"He's a big kid, a baby," said Clines, using the words as a compliment. "When he finally buckles down and gets serious about this game, there's no telling what kind of numbers he will put on the board. I don't think anybody's ever been as good at that age. He's in his own category. He is a natural."

As the season moved into May, Junior continued to provide thrills for Mariner fans. In fact, fans all over the league were buzzing about him and waited anxiously for the Mariners to come to town so they could see for themselves. By May 12, he was hitting a solid .303 with three homers and nine RBIs. On May 16, he slammed a two-run homer off Bill Wegman of Milwaukee in his first appearance as a pinch hitter. Then, on May 21, he legged out an inside-the-park homer off Clay Parker of the Yankees. On May 30, he walloped two homers in the same game against Jimmy Jones, also of the Yankees. His exploits were growing.

By early June he was already Seattle's newest hero. On June 4, the Mariners held Ken Griffey, Jr., Poster Day, giving a poster to all fans in attendance. All Junior did that day was homer off Charlie Hough of Texas. It was the first time he had faced a knuckleball pitcher and immediately blasted the floater, a pitch many hitters never solve.

When the All-Star break came in early July, Junior was on his way to a great rookie year. He was hitting a solid .279, had already slammed 13 home runs, and had driven in 38 runs. Among the Mariners, only veteran Jeffrey Leonard had more homers, with 15. His RBI total was third best on the club, while he also had 10 stolen bases, second to Harold Reynolds. In addition, he had made just three errors in the field during the team's first 81 games.

Though his name wasn't on the All-Star ballot, he still got some 79,051 write-in votes. It wasn't good enough to put him on the team, but it was the most write-in votes any player received and showed he was already a fan favorite. Now he looked forward to putting up even better numbers during the second half of the season.

Better yet, the Mariners had a 42–44 record at the All-Star break and looked to be in a position for at least a .500 season. After the break, Junior seemed more confident and better than ever. By July 24, his average was up to .287, tops among all American League rookies. He had 13 home runs and 45 RBIs. If he kept improving, some felt, he had a chance to perhaps hit .300, smack 25 home runs, and drive in 90 to 100 runs. That would equal a truly incredible rookie year. But that night, in a split second, everything changed.

The Mariners were in Chicago visiting the White Sox. After the game, Junior was showering in his hotel room. As he was stepping out of the shower he suddenly slipped. Instinctively, he threw out his right hand to keep from falling. But he went down anyway and the impact fractured a small bone that ran from his wrist to his little finger. He was placed on the disabled list immediately and would be out of the lineup for nearly a month. Everybody was devastated.

"[Junior's injury] is going to have an effect on a lot of things," Manager Lefebvre said, "from the team to the Rookie of the Year voting."

The Mariners had a number of other injuries as well, but Junior's was viewed as a major one. With the exciting rookie out of the lineup for most of August, the team nosedived. After flirting with .500 the entire season, the Mariners ended their hopes with a 9–20 mark in August and plunged back toward the bottom of the American League West.

Junior returned to the lineup on August 20, but it became apparent very quickly that he wasn't the same player. He wasn't as relaxed and seemed to be pressing, especially at the plate. It was as if he was trying to make up for lost time, something Manager Lefebvre confirmed.

"He was trying to catch up with the other Rookie of the Year candidates with one swing," the skipper said. "It wasn't surprising for a nineteen-year-old kid, really. He just lost his poise."

When he was forced to face reality, Junior admitted his manager was right.

"Yeah, I was worried about hitting the ball 700 feet," he said later. "I just wanted to reach 20 home runs."

It's an old adage in baseball that if you try to hit home runs, they just won't come. Junior was normally a very relaxed hitter with a picture-perfect swing. He would understand very soon that his natural swing was all he needed. As good as he was, the combination of his injury and pressing too hard when he returned really sabotaged his rookie year.

He was hitting a robust .287 before he was hurt. In the 39 games he played after returning to the lineup, he hit just .214. And in trying to hit home runs, he managed only three in 145 at-bats. The Mariners finished the 1989 season with a 73–89 record, sixth in their division. And Junior finished with good but not great numbers.

Playing in 127 games, he hit .264 with 16 home runs and 61 RBIs. He had 23 doubles and 16 stolen bases. And he showed a good batting eye, striking out just 83 times in 455 at-bats. But there were also some other facts you could glean from the numbers to once again confirm his great potential. For one thing, 13 of his 16 homers either tied the game or put the Mariners ahead. That's called hitting them when they count.

He was also fifth among American League outfielders with 12 assists. But again he was clutch: Six of his assists led to double plays, and that was the best in the league. In addition, he had amazed fans and teammates alike with his defensive abilities on more than one occasion. There was a game in Boston when he raced to the wall in left center to make a leaping grab of a Wade Boggs bid for an extra base hit. Just as he caught the ball he crashed into the "Green Monster," the wall at Fenway, but hung on to the ball.

In a Mariners game against the Milwaukee Brewers, Robin Yount hit a gapper to the wall in right center. Junior grabbed the carom and quickly saw Yount trying to go for a triple. He then let loose with a bullet throw that traveled to third on a line from the 375-foot sign in right, nailing Yount as he slid into the bag. There didn't seem to be anything he couldn't do.

Manager Lefebvre was right about one thing, however: The injury did cost Junior his chance for Rookie of the Year. He wound up third in the balloting as the prize was taken by relief pitcher Gregg Olson of Baltimore. But even Junior knew there would be plenty of time for awards.

As for his father, Ken, Sr., played the entire year with Cincinnati, appearing in part of all of 106 games. At age thirty-nine he batted .263 with eight homers and 30 RBIs in 236 at-bats. It certainly wasn't like the days of the Big Red Machine, but he did well enough to decide to come back again in 1990. During the season the two talked a number of times. Despite their very close relationship, their attitudes basically defined the generation gap.

"He's still nineteen," Ken, Sr., said of his son. "When he's out between the white lines, he's playing it as a game, and he's playing it hard. But when he comes home, he's nineteen."

As for Junior, he seemed to enjoy teasing Dad. "I basically go out and have fun," he said. "If [Dad] says something that I can relate to, then we'll talk. If not, I'll say, 'Yeah, yeah,' and he'll say, 'I know you're not listening.' It's a father-son thing."

Of course, the final piece of baseball advice came from the father. Said Ken, Sr., "I always told him that good things will happen if you're hitting the ball. But even if you're a lifetime .300 hitter, they are going to get you out seven of ten times. Where else can you be good one-third of the time and still be one of the best in the game?"

It wouldn't take Junior much longer to become one of the best in the game. And while that was happening, both he and his father would get an unexpected bonus, a real thrill they could cherish forever.

Chapter 5

Two Griffeys for the Price of One

In 1990, the Mariners began adding some new players they hoped would eventually join with Junior and help make the team a winner. Third baseman Edgar Martinez looked like a potential .300 hitter with a good glove. Outfielder Jay Buhner, who had come over from the Yankees a couple of years earlier, was thought to have real home run power. And six-foot-ten left-hander Randy Johnson, the tallest pitcher in baseball history, was looked upon as a potential big winner if he could get his blazing fastball under control. Having young players with all kinds of potential was what building a winner was all about.

At age twenty, Junior was considered the brightest of these collected talents and still a sure bet to become a bona fide superstar. Beginning his second season, he was still the youngest player in the majors. And with a year under his belt, he looked better than ever. In fact, he looked bigger. Though the media guide still listed him at six-foot-three, 195 pounds, it appeared to most that he was at least at the 200-pound mark.

And as soon as the season opened it became apparent that he was ready to accept the mantle as one of the game's best. In the first game on April 9, the Mariners were facing the California Angels at Anaheim. Pitching for the Angels was veteran righty Bert Blyleven, who had one of the best curveballs in the business.

Before the game, one of his teammates warned Junior about Blyleven's curve.

"Thanks," Junior said. Then, almost as an afterthought, he asked, "By the way, is Blyleven a righty or lefty?"

He not only didn't know what a lot of the pitchers threw, but didn't know who some of them were. Yet all he did against Blyleven that day was get four hits in five trips to the plate, including a three-run homer as the Mariners won, 7–4. He wasn't what they call a student of the game, but his natural ability was so great that he didn't have to be.

His fast start continued. He was named co–American League Player of the Week for the April 16–22 period in which he had 12 hits in 29 at-bats for a .414 average. He also clubbed two more homers and had 10 RBIs during that period. Four days later, on April 26, the Mariners were in New York for a game against the Yankees and Junior once again became a human highlight film with a catch that is talked about to this day.

To make the day more complete, Ken, Sr., had an off day with the Reds and came to New York to watch his son play a major league game for just the third time. Early in the game, Yankee right fielder Jesse Barfield came to bat with two outs and no one on base. Barfield had 199 career homers and was shooting for number 200, a milestone for any player. Junior was playing the powerful Barfield straight away and medium deep. Barfield got a pitch he liked and drove the ball high and deep into the nighttime New York sky. It was headed for the left center field wall . . . and so was Ken Griffey, Jr.

As with all great outfielders, Junior started running with the crack of the bat. He was running full speed as he felt the warning track beneath him. Then he took a quick glance at the eight-foot-high wall to gauge his distance and started his leap several yards away, looking almost like a long jumper. He sunk the cleats from his lead leg about halfway up the wall to aid his leap.

From the Seattle bullpen behind the wall, Mariners pitchers could see an arm flying high above and then over the top of the wall. As Barfield's long drive descended just behind the wall, Junior's glove got there. Just as suddenly as the Mariners pitchers saw his arm over the wall, it whiplashed back out of sight, taking the ball with it.

Junior landed with the ball in his glove and just began striding in toward the dugout as if the amazing catch had been routine. Left fielder Jeffrey Leonard rolled his eyes in total disbelief as Junior continued running toward the dugout with a huge grin on his youthful face. Even diehard Yankee fans were on their feet applauding as the Mariners came rushing out of the dugout to greet him with high fives. High up in the skyboxes, Yankee executives in attendance applauded.

Only Jesse Barfield, standing between first and second with his hands on his hips, looked angry. He had lost a bid for his two hundredth homer. And seeing his expression made Junior smile even more.

"That's why I like playing defense," he would say later, "because it's the only time I get to see somebody else but me get mad. As I jumped, I thought, I've got a chance. It's probably the best catch I ever made. It's the first one I've caught going over the wall, in practice or a game."

The reverberations from his catch continued. Up in the stands, a woman tapped Ken, Sr., on the shoulder and asked, "Is that your son?"

The senior Griffey smiled and nodded.

"Jesse Barfield's my husband," she said. But Maria Barfield couldn't help smiling as well. That's how captivating the moment had been.

Mariners coach Julio Cruz later said that the whole team had been affected by the catch.

"[Junior] shared that catch with all of us," Cruz remarked. "It pumped us all up."

And Manager Lefebvre could only shake his head in wonderment. "Every time he makes one of those plays, you think, 'He'll never top that one.' You can't believe how much it picks up the entire club. He's going to be one of the real marquee players in this league."

Pretty much everyone ended up happy that day. Barfield did get his 200th homer, slamming one his very next at-bat. But the Mariners won the game, 6–2, and Junior got a couple of hits to go with his great catch. Then late in the game Junior did something that only a few of his teammates noticed.

He was due up in the seventh inning. The Mariners had runners on first and second with two out when the Yanks made a pitching change. They brought in rookie reliever Alan Mills. While Mills warmed up, Junior stood in the on-deck circle, joking with teammate Pete O'Brien, laughing and looking at the people in the stands. He didn't even glance at Mills.

He wound up hitting a long fly to deep center which Roberto Kelly caught for the third out. It was an innocent enough thing, but Mariners catcher Scott Bradley saw more to it than just a long fly out.

"We had no scouting report on Mills, no one had ever faced him," Bradley said. "Griffey didn't even bother to check out his motion, didn't watch him warm up. Then he steps in and has a great at-bat."

Junior's answer was simple. "It just adds more pressure to know what a guy throws," he said. "You start looking for this or that, and all of a sudden he's snuck a 37-mile-per-hour fastball by you. I still can't tell you who's who. I don't know who's pitching. I don't even know the schedule.

But I don't really care. Whoever is pitching has still got to throw me something I can hit."

It was a basic philosophy. You go up, see the ball, and hit it. So far it was working beautifully for Junior. After the game, Ken, Sr., came into the locker room to congratulate his son. He shouted for Junior, but his son didn't hear him and walked into the showers.

"He ignores me now that he's bigger than me," Ken, Sr., teased.

Some veteran Yankee reporters reminded the senior Griffey of a great catch he had made when he played for the Yankees back in 1985 and had robbed Boston's Marty Barrett of a home run. Griffey smiled.

"I think I got higher than Junior did," he said, kidding around, with perhaps a bit of the competitive fire flaring up in him. But then he said the same thing about his son that others were saying.

"I'm in awe of him the same as you guys are. Yes, I'm a very proud dad."

By the following Sunday Junior had hit safely in 13 of his last 14 games and was leading the American League with a .395 average. He had also clubbed five homers and driven in 17 runs. A few days later he was named American League Player of the Month for April. He seemed on the way to a real super season. But for both Griffeys, the best was yet to come.

By All-Star break time Junior was still on his way to a great season. His batting average stood at .331, and he had 12 homers and 40 RBIs. He trailed only

Rickey Henderson (.335) in the batting race and was leading the league with 107 hits. Not surprisingly, he received 2,159,700 votes, second only to Jose Canseco of Oakland, and became the second-youngest player to start an All-Star Game. Al Kaline was a few months younger than Junior when he started back in 1955.

Though he didn't get a hit in the midseason classic, that would change dramatically in subsequent years. Now he began concentrating on the second half of the season. The Mariners were 43–41 at the break and everyone was hoping the team could have its first winning season ever.

By mid-August, Junior was still going strong. His average had dropped slightly to .323, but that was still second to Henderson. He also had 16 homers and 56 ribbys. With his great play in center, he was putting together a superstar season at age twenty. The one downer in his life was that his father was struggling badly in Cincinnati.

Ken, Sr., was being used sparingly by the Reds. He was hitting just .210 in 45 games, getting just 62 at-bats, and appearing mostly as a pinch hitter. He had just a single homer and only eight RBIs. The Reds were rebuilding and it was beginning to look as if there was no room for a forty-year-old part-timer who was just playing out the string. Then, on August 18, the Reds asked Griffey, Sr., to go on the disabled list so they could open a spot for a younger player. Ken simply refused, claiming he wasn't injured.

That left the Reds little choice. They put their

former star on waivers, which meant any club in either league could claim him. If no team wanted him, then they could give him his unconditional release. To the surprise of nearly everyone, the team that claimed him was the Seattle Mariners! The story made headlines all over the country. Now father and son would be playing together on the same team, another unprecedented first in baseball history.

Most people thought the move was little more than a publicity stunt, something Mariners management was doing to bring a few more fans to the ballpark. But Manager Lefebvre denied those stories vehemently.

"He [Griffey, Sr.] is not here so we can say we were the first to have a father and son on the same team," he said. "He's here to make a contribution on the field and in the clubhouse."

Ken, Sr., signed his Mariners contract on August 30, 1990. The next night he was in the starting lineup as Seattle hosted the Kansas City Royals in the Kingdome. Despite being in his eighteenth season, Ken, Sr., said he was nervous before the game. Junior was probably a bit nervous, too. Ironically, it was his father who was the "rookie" with the Mariners. Junior undoubtedly wanted his dad to do well.

As the Mariners took the field, Number 30 trotted out to left and Number 24 took his place in center. It was really an incredible sight. Though they were separated by nearly twenty years in age, both Griffeys stood in a major league outfield together, concentrating on the same thing—winning the game for their team. The feelings the two had must have been remarkable.

With more than twenty-seven thousand fans on hand, the game was routine for a few innings. Then came a moment no one would forget, especially the two Kens. Bo Jackson was up for the Royals. This was before the severe hip injury suffered by the two-sport star while he was playing football for the Los Angeles Raiders, the one that would also end his baseball career. Before the injury Jackson was one of the most powerful and fastest players in the game. Sure enough, he hit a shot down the left field line and took off.

Ken, Sr., raced toward the corner and grabbed the ball as it caromed off the wall. He quickly whirled around and fired hard toward second base. The throw was on the money. Second sacker Harold Reynolds took it and put the tag on the sliding Jackson. He was out!

The Kingdome crowd erupted in a huge roar. Out in center, Junior was grinning from ear to ear. He shouted over to his father, "Guess it runs in the family."

After the game, reporters clustered around the two Griffeys as they dressed side by side. Ken, Sr., talked about how exciting the moment had been for him.

"You can talk about the 1976 batting race, the two World Series I played in, and the All-Star games. But this is number one. This is the best thing that's ever happened to me. This is the pinnacle."

As for Junior, he had the view of the younger generation, without the same sense of history. He almost looked at it as part of growing up with Dad.

"It seemed like a father-son game," he joked, "like we were out in the backyard playing catch."

But in the Kansas City locker room, Bo Jackson reflected on the great throw that cost him a two-base hit.

"I didn't expect a perfect bounce and to have that old guy throw me out," he said, referring to Ken, Sr.'s age. "I'd have been mad if anyone else had thrown me out, but this was a piece of history."

Chapter 6

Settling in a Super Groove

It didn't take long for Ken, Sr., to show everyone that his signing wasn't just a publicity stunt. Playing alongside his son had given him renewed life. The Mariners won four of the first five games in which he played, as Senior got eight hits in 19 at-bats for a .421 average. He also drove home five runs. And in one game he had three hits.

"There was never a doubt in my mind that I could still do the job," Ken, Sr., said. "I usually wasn't in the lineup long enough with the Reds to get three hits."

But the Mariners had lost something of the edge as a team in early August, before Ken, Sr., joined them. They had a record of 10–18 for the month, which made it extremely unlikely that the team would get that elusive .500 season. And oddly enough, after his father joined the club, Junior went into a mild slump.

There were still some highlights. On September 14, Ken, Sr., came up in the first inning against Kirk McCaskill of the Angels at Anaheim and blasted a home run. Junior was the next hitter, so he stood at home plate waiting to congratulate his father. As soon as he touched home plate, the elder Griffey grinned at his son and said, "That's how you do it, son."

Not one to let his father grab all the family glory, Junior went after a 3-0 McCaskill fastball and also blasted it over the wall for back-to-back home runs.

Two days later, Junior came off the bench to pinch-hit in the ninth inning of another game against the Angels. California held a 2–0 lead with ace closer Bryan Harvey on the mound. But Seattle had two runners on base when Junior came up. He jumped on a Harvey delivery and slammed a long, three-run homer that would win the game for his team. Yet when the season ended the Mariners were in fifth place with a 77–85 record.

Junior had leveled off somewhat, but still produced a fine season. In 155 games he batted an even .300, hit 22 homers, and drove home 80 runs. He led the team in homers, RBIs, hits (179), and triples (7). He also won his first Gold Glove for fielding excellence, becoming the second youngest ever to earn that prize. Cincinnati catcher Johnny Bench was the youngest back in 1968.

As for Ken, Sr., he played in 21 games after

joining the Mariners and surprised everyone. He wound up batting .377 with three homers and 18 RBIs. He had played so well at age forty that he decided to come back for another year in 1991. That made Junior happy, as well.

The team also had some solid players now. Randy Johnson had gone 14–11 in 1990 and showed signs of being a big winner. Young starters Erik Hanson and Brian Holman also looked as if they would be solid pitchers. So the staff had a promising nucleus.

Junior, of course, was already the team's top hitter. Third sacker Edgar Martinez hit .302 in 1990 and was expected to get better. Young Jay Buhner would be given a solid shot in 1991 to develop into the power hitter he looked to be. Veterans Harold Reynolds, Alvin Davis, and Jeffrey Leonard were all proven hitters. Perhaps 1991 was the year the Mariners would finally crack the .500 barrier.

But before the regular season even started, there was some bad news. Ken, Sr., was in an automobile accident in March, suffering neck and back injuries that weren't serious, but might be enough to end his career. He would open the season on the disabled list.

"If I can't help the Mariners, I won't put the decision on their backs," he said. "I'll make it, and I'll make the right one." In other words, if he felt he couldn't play up to his standards, he would retire.

The Mariners lost their first six games, which led some disgruntled fans to feel that things would never get better. But with Junior leading the way and Ken, Sr., off the disabled list, the team began to win. By the end of April the club had rallied to a 12–13 mark, with Junior chipping away at a .319 clip and his father hitting .308 in a limited role. But at forty-one, Ken, Sr., could still do it. That in itself was amazing.

During the second half of May, Junior went into a batting slump that saw him go hitless in 18 straight at-bats, the worst slump of his career. His average fell from .343 to .292, yet the team won 15 of 27 games to move above the .500 mark. And, as is always the case with Junior, he didn't let his woes at the plate affect his fielding.

In a game against the Rangers on May 25, he raced into deep right center field to make a lunging, backhanded catch of a drive off the bat of Ruben Sierra. A split second after he caught the ball he crashed into the wall, but hung on. It was yet another incredible catch, the kind that were almost becoming routine.

Junior was still struggling at the plate somewhat in mid-June when he and the rest of the team learned that Ken, Sr., would have to go back on the disabled list with recurring neck problems from the auto accident in March. This time the problem was diagnosed as a ruptured disk. He would be out at least a month. Again, at his age, an injury like that could end his career.

At the All-Star break the Mariners were 40–42, still flirting with .500. Junior had still not gone on a tear and his average was .281. He had hit just nine homers and driven in 38 runs. They weren't bad numbers, but for a player looking for a real breakout season, they were somewhat disappointing.

Despite that, he led all American Leaguers in the All-Star balloting with 2,248,396 votes and got two hits in three trips to the plate as the A.L. won the game, 4–2. And once it was back to the business of the regular season, Junior came alive. He tied a club record with five hits in a July 18 game at Milwaukee. Five days later he hit his first-ever grand-slam home run, connecting with the bases loaded off lefty Lee Guetterman of the Yankees. A week later, he did it again, clearing the bases with another grand slam, this one off Roy Smith of the Orioles.

For the month of July, Junior batted .434, with five homers and 25 RBIs. Once again he was one of the most feared hitters in the league. The onslaught continued. He was American League Player of the Week for August 12–18, as he flailed away for a .542 average, with three home runs and nine RBIs. By the end of the month his average was up to .328, fifth in the batting race. He also had 17 homers and 72 RBIs, as well as 35 doubles, third best in the league. Suddenly he was putting together the superstar season everyone had predicted.

At this point there wasn't a better hitter in the big leagues. Manager Lefebvre also felt there wasn't a more valuable player.

"For what he's done for this club he definitely deserves MVP consideration," his manager said. "He's hitting well over .300, and if you could attach an average to his defense, he'd be hitting about .800."

Junior continued to play well right to the end. He whacked his third grand slam of the season on September 19 against Kansas City's Tom Gordon, and his twenty-second and final blast was an eleventh-inning shot that gave the Mariners a 10–8 victory over the White Sox at Chicago. On September 30, Junior drove in his one hundredth run of the season, becoming the twelfth youngest player to reach that milestone and the youngest since Al Kaline did it back in 1956.

Better yet, the Mariners finally cracked the .500 mark, finishing with an 83–79 mark. That didn't put them in the playoffs, but it was a start of something everyone hoped would continue. A number of the Mariners had fine seasons, but none was better than that of Ken Griffey, Jr.

He wound up with a batting average of .327, 22 homers for the second straight year, and an even 100 RBIs. In addition, he had 42 doubles and 18 stolen bases. His outfield play earned him a second straight Gold Glove and he was named to the Associated Press Major League All-Star team. But perhaps the most impressive, and frightening, aspect of his season was the numbers he put together after the All-Star break.

In the final 80 games of the season, Junior batted .372 with 13 home runs and 64 RBIs. To put up those numbers at age 21 only showed once more that his future was simply unlimited. The prevalent opinion was that he could only get better. He was just beginning to scratch the surface of his enormous potential . . . and that potential was to be an all-time great.

There was one other statistic that was very interesting. In his first three seasons, Junior had batted .264, .300, and .327. That made him the first and only player in baseball history to increase his batting average by 25 points or more in each of his first three years.

Then, shortly after the season ended, the natural progression of baseball came around, as it always does. Ken, Sr., had returned to play briefly in August and early September. But before the season ended he had to undergo surgery to repair the disk in his neck, the one injured in the auto accident. The combination of the injury and his age, forty-one, made him feel it would be too difficult to try to come back. He officially announced his retirement, finishing his nineteen-year career with a very solid .296 batting average. Ken, Sr., had been a real star for a number of years. Now his son was quickly becoming a superstar.

The family spotlight had been passed down to Junior. It was quite a tradition. If his career lasts as long as his father's, there will have been a Griffey playing in the majors for nearly forty consecutive years, which is a rather mind-boggling achievement. But Junior still had a long way to go.

Even though the Mariners had just produced their first winning season, the club made a managerial change, replacing Jim Lefebvre with Bill Plummer. The potential for improvement was still

Junior's follow-through is almost picture-perfect, as in this homer against the Yanks in 1995. *(AP/Wide World Photos)*

In June of 1987, 17-year-old Ken, Jr., was the number-one pick of the Seattle Mariners. *(UPI/Corbis-Bettmann)*

The Griffeys made baseball history in 1991 when they became the first father and son to play in the same outfield together. In this game at Yankee Stadium, Junior (with bat) hit third and Ken, Sr., batted cleanup. *(UPI/Corbis-Bettmann)*

By 1997, Junior was widely considered the best all-around player in baseball. His varied skills include speed on the basepaths, something even a slugger sometimes needs. *(AP/Wide World Photos)*

Ken, Sr., and Junior chat in the Seattle clubhouse after Junior made an incredible catch to rob Jesse Barfield of a home run on April 26, 1990. *(UPI/Corbis-Bettmann)*

A devoted family man, Junior celebrates son Trey's third birthday with a trip to Busch Gardens in Florida. *(AP/Wide World Photos)*

Unlike many of today's players, Junior willingly signs autographs and talks to fans both young and old. Here he takes time out during an exhibition game against the Southern League All-Stars in July of 1997. *(AP/Wide World Photos)*

Junior goes high over the wall at the KingDome trying to catch a home run off the bat of Cleveland's Carlos Baerga during the 1995 American League Championship Series. *(AP/Wide World Photos)*

This is the swing that had been described as the smoothest and sweetest in baseball. It resulted in one of Junior's record five home runs in the 1995 division playoff series against the Yankees. *(AP/Wide World Photos)*

Junior tracks another long blast. This one took place on May 20, 1997, against the Tigers. It was his 24th home run in a season that would see him hit a career-best 56. *(AP/Wide World Photos)*

there. Edgar Martinez hit over .300 again, while Jay Buhner began to blossom with 27 home runs. Both Randy Johnson and Brian Holman won 13 games and the team was solid up the middle with Omar Vizquel at short and Harold Reynolds at second.

But the season of hope turned quickly into one of disappointment. After a fairly good beginning in April, injuries to several starting pitchers took their toll. By the end of June the team was already 15 games below .500. The Mariners would never recover and limped home with a 64–98 record, dropping them to seventh and last in their division. Attendance at the Kingdome, which had topped two million for the first time in 1991, was down by nearly half a million fans. There was even talk of the team moving to another city.

As for Junior, his season was very close to 1991's, perhaps even a little stronger. He was on the disabled list for two and a half weeks in June with a sprained wrist and missed 20 games with various hurts. But he still managed to hit .308 with career bests of 27 homers and 103 runs batted in. He won his third straight Gold Glove for fielding excellence and was named to the *Sporting News* American League All-Star squad.

But the highlight of the year had to be the midseason All-Star Game. Voted a starter for the third consecutive year, Junior had three straight hits, including a home run off the Cubs' Greg Maddux. He was named the game's Most Valuable Player, making yet another first for the Griffey family. They were the first father-son combo to both be named MVPs of an All-Star Game and to hit a home run in that game.

But a bigger question was the direction the team would take from here. There were undoubtedly some fine players now supporting the superstar Griffey. Edgar Martinez had won the American League batting championship with a .343 average. Buhner had 25 home runs, and lefty Dave Fleming filled the pitching void with 17 victories. Big Randy Johnson still had trouble finding home plate and his wildness contributed to his 12–14 record. But the Big Unit, as he was called, led the American League with 241 strikeouts. Still, it wasn't nearly enough.

The front office took another step in the off-season when it named Lou Piniella the new manager. Sweet Lou, as he was called, had been a fine hitter during his playing days, and had managerial experience in both New York and Cincinnati. In fact, he had won a World Series with the Reds in 1990. Now his job was to turn the Seattle Mariners into a winning team.

Chapter 7

Breaking Out
Even More

The 1993 season was a turning point for the Seattle Mariners. And it was a turning point for Ken Griffey, Jr., as well. For one thing, he was married in the off-season. He had met his future wife, Melissa, several years earlier at a dance held at an under-twenty-one club, which both frequented because it was alcohol-free.

It was actually Melissa who asked Ken, Jr., to dance first. And it had nothing to do with his being a baseball star. When she first met him she didn't even know what a Seattle Mariner was. They were just two young people who were attracted to each other and had similar interests.

So Junior was certainly in a good frame of mind when the 1993 season started. The club suffered a severe blow, however, at the end of spring training when Edgar Martinez suffered a hamstring injury.

It wouldn't heal properly all year, limiting the defending A.L. batting champ to just 42 games and taking a big part of the Seattle offense out of the lineup.

But the opening-day lineup was still very solid. Vizquel was at short, veteran Mike Felder in left, Junior in center, young Tino Martinez batting cleanup at first, Pete O'Brien the designated hitter, Buhner in right, Mike Blowers at third in place of Edgar Martinez, Rich Amaral at second, and big Randy Johnson on the mound.

Playing before 55,928 fans at the Kingdome, the Mariners blew away the Toronto Blue Jays 8–1, giving Manager Piniella his first victory and, they hoped, getting the team off on the right track. While the team was better, flirting with the .500 mark all year, it was still apparent that they weren't quite ready for prime time. But the pieces were slowly beginning to fit.

Even without Edgar Martinez, the Mariners had a lot of offense. Tino Martinez, Buhner, Blowers, and O'Brien all had good home run power. And the leader of the pack, of course, was Ken Griffey, Jr. Once again, Junior had a breakout season, one that firmly established him as a premier slugger, a home run hitter who could go head to head with anyone.

As always, there were highlights. Like the 460-foot blast he hit off the Twins' Scott Erickson in the Kingdome on May 9. The ball hit and caromed down to the second deck. The mammoth shot left the home fans breathless. And when he connected off Billy Brewer of the Royals on June 15, Junior became the sixth youngest player in baseball history to reach 100 career home runs. But he was just getting started.

Once again he was the American League's top vote-getter for the All-Star Game, which was being played at brand-new Camden Yards in Baltimore. During the annual home-run-hitting contest, Junior became the first player to hit the B&O Warehouse, which was located behind the right field stands and across the street. It was another huge, 460-foot shot that did it. Junior finished second to Texas' Juan Gonzalez in the contest.

The Mariners had a 44–44 record at the All-Star break, but were becoming a team to be feared. Randy Johnson was finally cutting down on his bases on balls and becoming one of the most dominant pitchers in the league. And the hitters, led by Junior, could do damage at any time. The problems were the injury to Edgar Martinez and lack of depth in the pitching department. But Manager Piniella had moved the club in the right direction and everyone was beginning to feel that better days were close at hand.

Then, in July, Ken Griffey, Jr., reminded fans all over again just what a great ballplayer he had become. On July 18, he established a new record for American League outfielders by handling his 542nd consecutive chance without making an error. He would run the streak—which began on April 16, 1992—to 573 outfield chances before erring in an August 8 game with Texas. No wonder he won a Gold Glove every year.

Two days after establishing a new fielding record, Junior cracked a home run off Yankee reliever Paul Gibson in the eighth inning of a game in New York. In the next game, he hit another homer, then another in a third straight and then fourth straight game. Now there was a buzzing around the league. The record for home runs in consecutive games was eight, shared by Dale Long of the Pirates and Don Mattingly of the Yankees.

In that fourth game against Cleveland, Indians manager Mike Hargrove figured Junior was murdering them anyway, so he instructed catcher Junior Ortiz to tell Ken what pitch Albie Lopez would throw him. Knowing the pitch, Junior popped out. In his next at-bat, Ortiz didn't say anything and Junior homered. So much for knowing what pitch is coming.

In his next game, Junior blasted still another homer, his fifth straight game hitting one out. Then on July 25, he broke the Seattle record set by Richie Zisk back in 1981 when he connected off Cleveland's Jose Mesa. That made it six straight, and not surprisingly he was named co–American League Player of the Week with the Indians' Carlos Baerga. For the week, Junior had hit .400, blasted six home runs, and had nine runs batted in.

With six homers in six games already under his belt, Junior and the Mariners came home to host the Minnesota Twins on July 27. On the mound for the Twins was a tough righty, Kevin Tapani. Midway through the game Junior came up with the bases loaded. Tapani worked Junior carefully, but it still wasn't good enough. He picked out the pitch he wanted and blasted a grand-slam home run!

What a time to extend the streak. Not only was it his fifth career jack with the bases loaded, but it extended his homer streak to seven straight games, one short of the record.

Now the pressure mounted. Could Junior tie the record? The Mariners were playing the Twins once more and for seven innings Junior was homerless. Then he came up in the eighth against right-hander Willie Banks. It would probably be his last at-bat in the game. The crowd was almost hushed, but then erupted as Junior sent a rocket high and deep to right field. The ball slammed off the facing of the third deck for his eighth homer in eight games. He had done it!

Whenever he was questioned during the streak, Junior gave the same type of answer. He was trying to make the point that he didn't go up there looking to hit the ball out.

"I don't play to break records," he said. "I play to win ball games. I'm happier with a game-winning single than a home run if we lose."

But the next night some 45,607 fans came to the Kingdome with the anticipation of seeing history made. In fact, some 30,220 of them were walk-ins, people who bought their tickets on game day. Not surprisingly, they screamed and cheered with every move Junior made on the field. Junior certainly didn't have a bad night—but he didn't hit a home run.

The record book will show that Scott Erickson and Larry Casian were the pitchers who "stopped" Junior. The only thing they did was keep him from hitting one out. He banged out a single and a double in four at-bats. And the double was a line-drive rocket that could have gone out if Junior had gotten it up in the air.

In his final at-bat in the seventh inning, Casian hung a curveball, the kind of pitch a good hitter can jack out. Junior took that long, smooth, powerful swing . . . and popped up. He wouldn't hit a homer in a ninth straight game. Nevertheless, he had once again awed the baseball world.

"If he had hit a home run his last at-bat," Mariners pitcher Erik Hanson said, "the roof would have come off, and we'd have an outdoor stadium."

"I haven't seen him pop that pitch up in a month," added Manager Piniella. "But most people don't realize how hard it is to hit a ball out of the ballpark. If you hit eight in a month, that's 40-plus for a year."

And Junior had just hit eight in eight days. Now he looked as if he was headed for a 40-plus year. Up to this point, the most he had hit was 27. Tall and slim-looking, despite the fact that he now weighed about 205 pounds, he still didn't look like a proto-type home run hitter. He was more Henry Aaron than Babe Ruth. He tried to explain where the power came from.

"Most of the other [top home run hitters] just have to use their big butts and big python arms to hit homers," he said. "Me, I'm the little guy in the group. You don't really have to be strong. You have to be quick. You have to trust your hands. If you can keep your eye on the ball as it leaves the pitcher's hand, your hands will automatically take you where the ball is going. You can hold the bat any way you want. Just be comfortable.

"And you can't go up there thinking home run. If you do, you may be lucky to hit one out of 10 out [of the park]."

As the Mariners continued their quest to finish over .500, Ken Griffey, Jr., continued to put together his greatest season. When he slammed his thirty-third homer on August 10 off Tom Gordon at Kansas City, he broke Gorman Thomas's all-time Mariners record. But he wasn't about to stop there. He showed once again how explosive he could be in successive games on August 25 and 26.

Facing right-hander Bill Gullickson at Detroit on the twenty-fifth, he blasted a pair of long homers. Returning to the Kingdome the next night, Junior promptly whacked two more, this time off Dave Stewart of Toronto. Less than a week later, on September 1, he slammed his fortieth of the year, this one off Mike Moore of Detroit. Not only was he the first Seattle player ever to hit 40 in a season, but he was the tenth youngest player in history to reach that milestone.

And when he drove in his 100th run of the season on September 13, he became the fourth youngest player ever to have three, 100-RBI seasons. Are you beginning to get the picture? Ken Griffey, Jr., was simply becoming a super ballplayer. And he was still just twenty-three years old.

The Mariners finished the 1993 season with an 82–80 record, a bit disappointing, but at least the team was above .500 again. Maybe they could build upon it. Buhner was becoming a top-flight slugger with 27 homers and 98 RBIs, while big Randy Johnson finally became a real force. The Big Unit had a 19–8 record with a major league best 308 strikeouts. There was little doubt that the Mariners finally had an ace, a go-to guy on the mound who intimidated hitters.

But the real star of the 1993 Seattle season was Ken Griffey, Jr. He simply kept outdoing himself. Junior batted .309, with 45 home runs and 109 RBIs. He trailed only Juan Gonzalez of Texas and Barry Bonds of the Giants for the major league lead in dingers. They had 46 each. In addition, he was voted by the players to the *Sporting News* All-Star team and won a fourth consecutive Gold Glove. In the outfield, there was no one better.

Perhaps, however, the day Junior enjoyed the most in 1993 came on May 21 at Kansas City. The Royals held a promotion called Turn Back the Clock day, the players appearing in old-style uniforms. That day, Junior took the field not wearing his usual number 24. Instead he wore a uniform with number 30 on his back, just another way to show his respect and his thanks to his father. To Ken, Jr., it would always be a father-son thing.

Chapter 8

Can Anything Stop Junior?

Baseball has as great a tradition as anything in America. It is a national rite of spring that baseball teams flock to Florida, Arizona, and California to begin preparations for yet another season. It happens every year, no matter what else is transpiring in the world. And players from every team head to warm weather filled with hope and anticipation. During spring training, everyone has visions of a World Series in October.

Coming off a winning season (though by just two games), the Mariners again had high hopes in 1994. Maybe this would be the breakout year, the year the team seriously contended for a playoff spot. As for Junior, he was just twenty-four years old yet already considered one of the best all-around players in the game. Maybe only the Giants' Barry Bonds had all-around skills equal to Junior's.

In 1994, Junior came to spring training with a special glow on his face. On January 19, his wife Melissa had given birth to their first child, a son they named Trey Kenneth Griffey. It gave Junior a whole new perspective on his life.

"Every day, I pinch myself and say I can't believe I have a baby," he said. "He's mine. You could take away baseball, take away all my material things, but I would still have him. That means everything to me."

To Junior, a whole new world had opened up, and he was doing things that he considered tougher than hitting a fast-breaking slider.

"Changing diapers," he said, "now that's rough. When I change his diaper he picks up one leg, and when I push it down, he picks up the other. It's hard work. He's so little. I just don't want to drop him and break him."

When someone reminded him that his hands had helped him win four straight Gold Gloves, Junior answered quickly, "Well, these hands are still a little shaky when it comes to Trey."

It was unusual to hear a baseball star speak so tenderly about his relationship with his infant son. But before 1994 ended, people would know more about Ken Griffey, Jr., than ever before. To this point, Junior had not been the most talkative of players. He was always friendly and courteous when interviewed, never surly or short-tempered, like so many modern athletes. But by the same token, he never sought out the limelight. He preferred to let his skills on the ball field do the talking for him.

But now he had reached a point where his star

was shining so brightly that he could no longer remain in the background. During the off-season, he also had a part in the movie *Little Big League*. In the film, Junior played himself, but he did it with a naturalness that impressed the movie people.

"He has a real screen presence," said Andy Scheinman, the film's director. "When he's on the screen, your eyes just naturally go to him. He's like Tom Cruise in that sense. We had a number of big-time ballplayers in the movie, but when Griffey was on the field, it was like a different world. He is just a huge, huge star."

One reason for Junior's increasing popularity was his friendly demeanor and his off-field image. Unlike many of today's athletes, there were no scandals, no after-hours problems of being somewhere he shouldn't have been. Now that he was a family man, there was more gloss to his image than ever before. Asked how he avoided the many traps athletes can fall into, Junior said, "I have always been able to stay away from that stuff. My parents told me from the beginning, I could be a ballplayer or I could be a what-if. I have pride in myself, pride in my family, and pride in my teammates. I wouldn't want to do anything to jeopardize any of those three."

In addition to his growing family, Junior's entry into the world of endorsements was growing. During the 1993 season he had signed a large deal with Nintendo, the video-game manufacturer. In April 1994 the company introduced a new game: *Ken Griffey, Jr., Presents: Major League Baseball*. It was backed by a $4 million advertising campaign.

In addition, he was also endorsing Franklin batting gloves, Rawlings fielding gloves, Louisville Slugger bats, and Upper Deck trading cards.

And he also had a contract with Nike, which would start a big campaign with him during 1994.

"We feel like Ken is going to be as big a star as baseball has ever seen," said Terdema Ussery, the president of Nike Sports Management. "Ken is the type of person that kids can love and adults can respect. He is a true role model, and that is something baseball sorely needs."

Though no one knew it at the time, baseball would need Junior more than ever in the upcoming years. That assessment would be based on events that would take place late in the 1994 season. At the beginning of that season, there was great anticipation. For the first time there were three divisions in each league, which changed the playoff format. Instead of the two divisional winners in each league meeting to decide which team went to the World Series, there would now be three divisional winners plus the team with the best second-place record as a wild card entry all making the postseason.

That gave baseball an extra round of playoffs, similar to sports like football, basketball, and hockey. It was a big change, but one that would give more teams a chance at getting to the World Series. That allowed teams such as the Mariners renewed hope. Seattle was now in a four-team Western Division with Texas, Oakland, and the Angels. As for Junior, the way things began in 1994, it looked as if he was going to rewrite the record book.

The highlights began coming early. On April 9, he had the eleventh two-homer game of his career, connecting off Juan Guzman of the Blue Jays. On April 24, he won a game with a clutch three-run homer in the eighth inning off Brad Pennington of the Orioles. The ball landed on Eutaw Street, some 438 feet from home plate, the longest homer ever hit by a left-handed batter at Camden Yards in Baltimore.

By the end of April, Junior had set a club record by driving home 20 runs. But the team was disappointing with a 10–13 record, again struggling just to maintain a mark close to .500. Then, when Junior homered off Tony Fossas of the Red Sox at Fenway Park in Boston on May 3, he had completed a cycle. He had now homered in every single American League city during his career.

In mid-May, he went on one of his patented batting tears, the kind that normally carries a team. For 11 games, from May 14 to 24, Junior hit as well as anyone who has ever played the game. He had 19 hits in 37 at-bats for a .514 average. He not only hit safely in every game during the tear, but also walloped nine homers and drove home 13 runs in that span.

He reached yet another milestone on May 20, when he hit the 150th home run of his career off Texas' Roger Pavlik at the Kingdome. At the age of twenty-four years and five months, he was the third youngest player ever to reach 150 homers. Only Mel Ott, who hit his 150th home run at 23 years and 6 months, and Eddie Mathews, at 23 years and 10 months, had reached that number at a younger age. And all of baseball began taking notice at the end of May when Junior already had 22 home runs. The most home runs ever hit by the end of May had been 20, by Mickey Mantle in 1956. Now there was talk of Junior breaking Roger Maris's all-time record of 61 homers in a season.

Unfortunately, all was not well with the Mariners. The high hopes of spring had dissolved with an 11–16 May that left the team with a 21–29 record after two months. Randy Johnson was pitching well again, while Jay Buhner and Tino Martinez were helping Junior in the power department. But Edgar Martinez wasn't fully recovered from his severe hamstring injury of a year earlier, and the pitching wasn't deep enough. Plus the bullpen and overall team defense were still wanting. Finally, Junior boiled over for the first time in his career.

He ripped his teammates for a lack of heart and told people he didn't see himself staying with the Mariners once his contract expired at the end of 1996. Though he somewhat tempered his remarks after his initial outburst, it was still apparent that what he wanted most was to play on a winning team.

"It was something I felt at the time, and I'm not sorry I said it," he reiterated a short time later. "What I regret is that I didn't choose my words carefully enough. I didn't mean heart. This team has heart. But just going out and playing is not enough. Winning is what matters."

As he moved deeper into his career, all the individual praise didn't really matter. He knew he would always be the best player he could be, giving

100 percent every time he was on the field. But great players also leave their mark by playing for championships, and it was undoubtedly beginning to weigh on Junior as he saw other top players in postseason action. Yet the Mariners didn't seem to be getting any closer.

"[Building a winning team] is always out of my hands," he said. "That's the frustrating thing. If some of the guys around here don't improve, they won't be here next year. That's the way the game is, and that's how it has to be."

Nevertheless, Junior continued his personal onslaught. On June 13 at Texas, he hit a grand slam off Bruce Hurst of the Rangers and had a career-high six runs batted in. The next day he hit two more homers, including the game-winner in the thirteenth inning. A day later he smacked another dinger, this one off Kevin Brown, the 161st of his career. He was now the Mariners' all-time home run hitter. And by the end of June, the talk about Junior making a run at Maris's record really intensified. He now had a record 32 homers by the end of baseball's third month. The previous record through June was 30, set by the legendary Babe Ruth in both 1928 and 1930.

When the first half of the season ended, Junior had a .329 batting average with 33 home runs and 69 runs batted in for 87 games. He was on his way to his greatest season. The fans knew it, too. Junior was voted to the All-Star Game starting lineup for the American League for a fifth straight year. Only this time he received an incredible 6,079,688 votes, by far a new record. The previous mark was 4,292,740 votes received by Hall of Famer Rod Carew in 1977.

The day before the game itself, Junior thrilled the crowd at Three Rivers Stadium in Pittsburgh by winning the annual home-run-hitting contest. He jacked seven balls into the seats as the crowd cheered. With many former stars on hand, Junior had a chance to talk with some of the all-time greats, and they with him. Reggie Jackson, known to fans as Mr. October for his exploits in the postseason, spent a good deal of time talking with Junior.

"We love Ken Griffey, Jr.," Reggie would say, "because he is everything we would like to be. He's young, he's good-looking, he's got the best smile in the world, and he's a heroic athlete. He makes people feel welcome. He genuinely enjoys making people happy or making them laugh. There are a lot of players who are the opposite— they go out of their way to scare people off.

"Junior is a shot in the arm for baseball. He is what this game needs right now. He is creating excitement and making headlines just by his presence. There hasn't been anyone like that since . . . Reggie Jackson."

No one would ever accuse Reggie of being overly modest. But his statement may have been true. Lou Piniella, who played alongside Jackson and now managed Griffey, talked of a fundamental difference between the two greats.

"Reggie was what I would classify—in a nice way—as a villain when he was playing," Piniella explained. "People came out to root against him.

With Kenny, people come out to root for him, to be swept up by his enthusiasm and amazed by his talent. But what [Reggie and Junior] share, and this is what makes them special, is the same ability to turn the fans on."

That was apparent by the fact that Junior had 1.8 million more fan votes for the All-Star Game than any other player in either league. Even White Sox first baseman Frank Thomas, a young player who rivals Junior as a hitter, though not as an all-around player, acknowledged that he would never have the widespread popularity of Griffey.

"The thing about Junior," said Thomas, "is that he has that golden smile. He is like a kid on the sandlot. We're all competitors, we all play to win, but he always seems to be having more fun than the rest of us."

Having fun on the ball field was always a priority with Junior, but he also felt his hard work and all-out style of play was what had brought him to the high level he had achieved.

"I've always felt like it isn't the fans or the press that makes you a big star," he said. "You have to play yourself to that level. Before, I wasn't real comfortable doing commercials or being in the spotlight, because I wanted to establish myself on the field."

At the All-Star Game, Griffey had two more hits, including a double and an RBI. That gave him eight hits in 14 at-bats for a .571 average in five All-Star contests. Junior aimed to please, no matter what the occasion.

Then shortly after the All-Star break it was revealed that Junior and his family had been going through something that can often turn into a nightmare. In June, Ken was alerted by the FBI that someone had made a threat on his life, as well as on the lives of his wife, Melissa, and son, Trey. The threat was made in the form of a note, which found its way into FBI hands. This is something that happens with professional athletes (as with other public figures, such as actors and politicians) from time to time. Most often it is the work of a crackpot who never even tries to follow through. But threats such as this must be taken seriously and are also very unnerving.

"I understand things like this come with being who I am," Junior said, this time not flashing his winning smile. "There are crazy people in this world. That's why I'm not a public person. When I want you to see me is when I'm at the ballpark. That's it. It's bad enough that people have found out where I live, but they also know when I'm gone, too. It's in the paper every day."

To be extra cautious, Junior said he never allows public pictures of him with his wife and son. His home, which was located some twenty-five miles from Seattle, was protected by a security gate and four rottweilers. Also, four boyhood friends living in the Seattle area helped give him and his family more of a sense of security. It's unfortunate when a great athlete like Junior has to worry about his and his family's safety, but it is sometimes part of being famous.

After the All-Star break the Mariners' woes continued despite Junior's great play. There was a game with the Yanks that the Mariners lost even though Junior slammed two homers and a double, drove in five runs, and made a circus catch in center. It marked the second game in a row the Mariners had scored eight runs and still lost.

"It's rough, very rough," was all Junior could say. "These things are going to happen. But it seems like they're always happening to us."

On July 23, Junior blasted his thirty-sixth homer of the year against the Boston Red Sox. He still had an outside chance of catching up with the record of 61. But by this time there was something else on the horizon, something no one wanted to see happen. The Players' Union and owners were deadlocked in contract negotiations and the players had set a deadline for a strike. If there was no real progress or a settlement, they said they would go on strike after the games of August 11. If that happened, the rest of the season would be in jeopardy.

It must have been tough for the players to go about business as usual with the strike looming. And while Junior was having a great July, the Mariners had just a 7–18 record, playing themselves out of contention as well as losing sight of a possible .500 season. Then, at the beginning of August, most players were being asked more questions about a possible strike than about the action on the field.

"Everybody thinks that if we strike the season's going to be over," Junior said, when asked. "I don't want to believe that. They'll still have some time to discuss things before a final decision has to be made."

Like many other players whose salaries were

well in excess of a million dollars a year, Junior was asked if perhaps the players were getting greedy, that by striking despite huge salaries, they would alienate the fans, many of whom were just working people struggling to make a living.

"We're just trying to protect the young guys, help them get the same opportunities that we've had," Junior said. "If we strike, some of the players could lose more than a million dollars in salary. What about that? Some will lose more because of incentive bonuses. So a lot of money is going to be lost . . . that we can't make up. We have families that we have to provide for, and we do it the best way we know how, and that's by playing baseball. But this strike isn't about us. It's about the guys coming up in the future.

"The post office has a union. They go on strike. The bus drivers have a union and they go on strike. That affects other people's lives. We affect other people as far as enjoyment is concerned. It's tough in our situation because people think because we make millions of dollars that we're greedy. But we're just trying to help out the guys who are going to be in the big leagues in two or three years."

Junior said that the higher-salaried players on the Mariners told some of the younger players that they would help them out if necessary. But the possibility of a strike brought out many different opinions. The players knew if there was a strike that many fans would call them greedy. Yet they believed in their cause and their union. So the deadline continued to loom.

As he tried to concentrate on baseball, Junior

continued to be met with distractions. At one point, an opposing manager, Buck Showalter of the Yankees, criticized him for wearing his baseball cap backward while sitting in the dugout or warming up before a game. Showalter said it disrespected the uniform. It was also the way many young kids wore baseball-style caps on the streets.

Junior defended it as something he always had done. "I've always worn my hat on backwards since I was little," he said. "My dad's hat was too big for me to wear it forward, so I'd turn it around and wear it backwards. You can ask anyone in my family. It has nothing to do with disrespect for the uniform. Even when I go to the store and try on a hat, I always put it on backwards."

The irony of the 1994 season was that with the distraction of the strike at the beginning of August, the Mariners suddenly began to play their best baseball of the year. They won nine of their 10 games. That tenth game of the month was played on August 11. And all Junior did that day was blast a grand-slam home run off Ron Darling of the A's. It was his fortieth home run of the year, and seventh grand slam of his career.

By winning nine of 10 games, the Mariners raised their record to 49–63, still extremely disappointing. With 50 games remaining, some thought they might be able to build something for the next year. And, hey, if Junior got hot . . . well, 22 homers in 50 games wasn't unheard of. Maybe he could still get those 62 home runs and break the record.

But none of that was to be. Last-minute negotiations between the players and owners fell apart. As promised, the players went on strike at midnight. There were no games on August 12. At first everyone thought the strike would be settled quickly. After all, the owners certainly wouldn't want to put the postseason in jeopardy, especially not in the first year of the new playoff setup.

But neither side would give an inch. The strike dragged on—one week, then two, and then it was September. Finally, on September 14, the owners decided there was nothing more they could do. They abruptly canceled the season. There would be no more baseball in 1994. No playoffs, no World Series, and no more games for players like Ken Griffey, Jr., to go after any records. It was over!

For the abbreviated year, Junior had played in 111 games. He hit .323, led the American League with 40 home runs, and drove home 90 runs. Despite the stopping of the season, individual awards were still given. Not surprisingly, Junior won a fifth straight Gold Glove and was named to the Associated Press Major League All-Star team.

But the strike led to an unsatisfactory ending for everyone. There was no World Series for the first time since 1904. And while it was the eighth work stoppage in 22 years, it was the first one that caused the cancellation of the postseason. In addition, the fan perception that millionaire ballplayers were no more than greedy brats led some to make dire predictions about the popularity of the game when it resumed.

As for the Mariners and Ken Griffey, Jr., the strike came just as the team seemed to be playing better baseball. But the 49–63 losing season was another bitter disappointment, even before the stoppage. The team had been in existence for 18 years now, with just two winning seasons. They were a team with arguably the best all-around player in baseball in Junior Griffey, and with arguably the most dominant pitcher in the game in Randy Johnson.

The Big Unit was 13–6 in the strike-shortened season, leading the league in strikeouts (204 in 172 innings), complete games (9), and shutouts (4). There were also some solid supporting players. This was a team that, by rights, should be turning it around. Now everyone looked to 1995 as the year it might happen.

And what about Junior? For most of 1994, it looked as if nothing could stop him. What finally did wasn't good pitching or great defense. Not even a batting slump. It was a players' strike. It stopped what would undoubtedly have been Junior's greatest season. He could only hope that 1995 would be different, especially for the team. As he had said on so many occasions, "I don't play to break records; I play for the Seattle Mariners."

Chapter 9

Balancing the Bad
with the Good

The Players' Association–owners deadlock proved a tough nut to crack. During the elongated off-season, there were long periods of time in which the two sides didn't even bother to negotiate. As unbelievable as it sounds, suddenly the start of the 1995 season was in jeopardy. Would there be a spring training in March? There was always spring training. It was an American tradition. Some people even began asking if baseball would ever come back.

It would turn out to be the longest work stoppage in the history of professional sports, lasting 234 days. Before the strike ended, major league teams went to spring training as usual, but without the regular players. Replacement players were hired. And when the strike finally ended, it was agreed to delay the start of the season until the regular players were ready. So the 1995 season wouldn't begin until the end of April and would be shortened to 144 games, 18 fewer than usual.

And perhaps the final irony of the strike was that the issues that caused it were still unresolved. The two sides still didn't have a collective bargaining agreement. That would come later. Logically speaking, it was a strike that didn't have to happen. But, unfortunately, logic doesn't always take precedence. Most of the players were simply happy to be back doing what they did best. Now the question was how many of the fans would return.

This was an especially important issue in Seattle. Attendance had never been great but the Mariner ownership wanted a new stadium and hoped the fans and the city would help underwrite it. After 1995 there would be just two years remaining on the Kingdome lease and Mariner ownership talked of putting the team up for sale and suggesting the new owners look to move it to another city . . . unless a new stadium was built.

When the regular players arrived for a belated spring training, John Ellis, the Mariners' chief executive officer, gathered the players around, told them to forget about the strike, then suggested they win their division so the team could have a chance to get themselves a new stadium.

"Do you know what kind of pressure that is?" asked right fielder Jay Buhner. "Knowing that if you don't win, the team is going to skip town? That the future of the franchise is on your shoulders? Man, that's pressure."

Because the team wasn't making a lot of money, there were also thoughts of cost-cutting. Rumor had it that either Randy Johnson or designated hitter Edgar Martinez would be traded in an effort to cut the payroll. But General Manager Woody Woodward and Manager Piniella finally prevailed upon the front office to leave the team intact, pointing out that if they wanted to try to save baseball in Seattle, the star players would have to stay.

The Mariners finally opened the 1995 season on April 27, facing the Detroit Tigers in the Kingdome. Randy Johnson was on the mound and the rest of the opening-day lineup certainly appeared to have the firepower to compete against anyone.

Darren Bragg was in left field, newly acquired Joey Cora at second. Junior opened in center, with Buhner batting cleanup and playing right. Edgar Martinez was the designated hitter, with Tino Martinez at first, Mike Blowers at third, and Felix Fermin at short. This was a lineup that figured to score runs in bunches. And when Randy Johnson twirled a three-hit shutout to open the season—the Mariners winning, 3–0—the team was off to a good start. Especially since all three runs came on a Ken Griffey, Jr., home run off Detroit's Sean Bergman. The team's two biggest stars shone in the victory.

Two nights later, Junior thrilled the fans again. This time he caught a David Wells fastball just right and blasted a moon shot that went into the third deck in right field at the Kingdome. It was estimated that the ball would have traveled some 462 feet had it not hit the stands. Once again, Junior appeared poised on the brink of a super season.

His pace slowed somewhat in early May, but at least the team had jumped off to a winning record.

While Junior's power numbers were good, his average was down around the .260 mark. Everyone was just waiting for one of his patented batting tears. It was bound to come.

On May 26, the Mariners were hosting the Orioles at the Kingdome. Baltimore's Kevin Bass was up and launched a long drive toward deep right center field. As always, Junior was off with the crack of the bat. He raced back at full speed while tracking the flight of the ball. He didn't stop as he reached the warning track. At the last second, he reached across his body with his right arm, extended as far as he could, and made another brilliant catch a split second before crashing into the wall. He tried to break the impact with his left hand. Unfortunately, the impact wasn't the only thing he broke.

Junior trotted off the field in obvious pain and didn't return. When the news filtered back from the hospital, it was devastating to the team. He had fractured both bones in his left wrist, a very serious injury, especially for a hitter who depends on his wrists for so much of his power.

The next day, Junior underwent three hours of surgery, the operation performed by hand specialist Dr. Ed Almquist and team physician Dr. Larry Pedegana. The injury was so severe that the doctors had to put a four-inch metal plate and seven screws in the wrist to hold the bones in place. It was estimated that Junior would be sidelined for three months. With that timetable, he would return around September 1, in time for the stretch run—if the Mariners were in a position to make a stretch run.

At the time of his injury, he was hitting .263 with seven homers and 15 RBIs in 27 games. Over a full 162-game schedule those power numbers put him on a pace for 42 homers and 90 RBIs, which would be slightly below his norm. In addition, his batting average was more than 40 points lower than his career mark. That's why everyone was waiting for him to get hot. Now the wait would be considerably longer.

"This is something that happens in baseball," said Junior. "Naturally, I'm disappointed. I feel I'm letting everyone down by not being able to play. I'll just have to follow doctors' orders and try to rehab the wrist as fast as I can. I definitely plan to play again this year."

For the first time since Junior's rookie year of 1989, the Mariners would have to play a long stretch of games without their star center fielder. The effect of this kind of situation can go in one of two ways. The other players can get down, feel they can't win without the big man, and go into a funk. Or they can find a determination to win no matter what and raise their own games to the next level.

The Mariners had a 19–13 record at the end of May, trailing the California Angels in the American League West. Several players were already showing signs of putting together their best years. Edgar Martinez was all the way back from his injuries of two years earlier and battling for the league lead in hitting. Jay Buhner was slugging away at a pace that could put him between 35 and 40 homers. First baseman Tino Martinez also looked on the brink of becoming a bona fide power hitter.

On the mound, Randy Johnson was all but unbeatable. The problem, however, continued to be the starters behind him as well as the bullpen. Pitching was definitely the Mariners' Achilles' heel. If it didn't improve, they were in trouble once more.

June and July proved to be tough months for the Mariners. Still reeling from Junior's injury, the team did seem to go into a funk in June, compiling just an 11–17 record, dropping them to .500 for the year. It looked like the same old Mariners all over again. In July, the club played a bit better, but still had a 13–14 month, giving them a 43–44 record on the year. The Cal Angels had a big lead in the A.L. West, making a first-place Mariners finish seem unrealistic. But because of the strike in 1994, this was now the first year that a wild card team could make the playoffs, and the Mariners didn't throw in the towel.

On July 31, the team made a trade that brought another proven starter in right-hander Andy Benes to Seattle. Two weeks earlier, the Mariners had acquired lefty reliever Norm Charlton, thought already past his prime. But Charlton regained his form and gave the team a reliable closer. On August 2, the Mariners still trailed the Angels by 13 full games. Only two teams in baseball history had ever come back from a deficit of 13 or more at that point in the season to win a league or division championship.

The outside chance of a wild card kept the players from giving up. "No doubt about it," said General Manager Woody Woodward. "If there's no wild card, we would have gone into a mode you've seen in years past. Move some salaries and getting young talent in exchange.''

But this time the team stood pat. They also had some more good news. Word was that Junior was ahead of schedule with his rehab and could join the club around the middle of the month instead of at the end of September. That also spurred the players to work hard to stay in the race.

''Getting Junior back is going to be like an acquisition,'' said Randy Johnson. ''Like, hey, we just picked up Ken Griffey on the waiver wire.''

In other words, it would be an unexpected bonus. The team had been playing without Junior for two months. They began to play a little better in early August, especially when they got word that Junior had targeted August 15 as his return date. He received clearance from the doctors and would resume playing with the metal plate and screws still embedded in his injured wrist. It was hard to imagine him being at full strength, but any contributions from Junior had to help.

After playing one game at Tacoma of the Pacific Coast League to get ready, Junior rejoined the Mariners at Minnesota.

''It's good to be back,'' Junior said. ''There's never been a summer before when I haven't played baseball and it hasn't been easy. Nor has it been easy watching the team struggle and not being able to do anything about it. Hopefully, now I will.''

By the time he returned, Junior had missed 73 games. During that time, the Mariners were just 36–37, a game under .500. In the eyes of most, that was the same old Mariners. Junior played against Minnesota and got one hit in four trips to the plate. But the Mariners lost, and that defeat left them 12 and a half games behind the Angels.

The next night Junior had a single off Frankie Rodriguez of the Twins, the 1,000th hit of his career. He was the seventh youngest player in history to reach that milestone. His first home run in his comeback came on August 20, off Rheal Cormier of Boston. That was probably the best news. The wrist was holding up and the power was still there. But when the Mariners hosted the New York Yankees on August 24, the team had lost four of five games. Their record was now 54–55. Not only were they still far behind the Angels, but they were also four games behind Texas in the A.L. West and in the race for the wild card spot. In fact, the Yanks, who trailed Boston in the A.L. East, were also in the hunt for the wild card.

Before the game, the Mariners' players held a closed-door meeting, trying to spur each other on. But that night the pitching faltered again, and going into the ninth inning Seattle was down by one, 7–6. The Yanks had their relief ace, John Wetteland, on the mound trying to close it out. Wetteland got the first two Mariners and it didn't look good. Seattle had trailed after eight innings in 43 previous games and lost them all.

Speedy Vince Coleman, who had been acquired on August 15, worked Wetteland for a walk. With Joey Cora up, Coleman wasted no time in stealing second. Then he gambled again and stole third. On the next pitch, Cora hit a soft liner that shortstop

Tony Fernandez jumped for, but the ball went off his glove, Coleman scoring to tie the game as the crowd went wild.

They got even louder when Junior stepped up with a chance to win it. Figuring Junior's bat might still be a tad slow because of his long layoff, Wetteland tried to throw an inside fastball past him. Junior jumped on it with the same sweet stroke he had been using since 1989. He connected with the fat part of the bat and the ball rocketed on a line toward the right field seats. Junior knew it was gone from the instant he hit it. He thrust his arms over his head and raised both index fingers as he began circling the bases to a thunderous ovation. The Mariners had won the game, 8–6, and they had done it in the best way possible.

"That was the one that got us going," Manager Piniella said. "It wasn't just how we did it, but because Junior did it. We had him back."

Chapter 10

Mariner Mania

Beginning with the game against the Yanks and Junior's dramatic home run, the Mariners suddenly began playing great baseball. They were winning games that they had always lost before—coming from behind, getting solid relief pitching, finding a different hero each night. At the same time, the California Angels began losing, slumping badly. Their lead began to shrink.

And as the Angels' lead shrunk, more and more fans began flocking to the Kingdome. The Mariners never had a huge following in Seattle, but then again they were never really winners. Now the team had a new catchphrase. REFUSE TO LOSE signs began appearing all over the Kingdome. And as the crowds increased, so did the noise level. Visiting teams had trouble winning there.

"You can feel the electricity there," said Randy Johnson. "The fans have been so boisterous. When there are nineteen thousand fans here, they make the noise of fifty thousand. When there are fifty thousand, it sounds like a quarter of a million."

"This is what it's all about," Junior said, as the Mariners continued to gain ground. "This is what I've been waiting for ever since my rookie year."

The Mariners continued to gain ground in almost miraculous fashion. When someone at the Kingdome decided to keep track of the wild card race by hanging the contending team banners in the order of their records, a number of players objected. They were no longer thinking just wild card. They were thinking division title.

"I didn't want us to sell ourselves short," Jay Buhner said, "to settle for shooting for the wild card. You compete to win, to finish first. If we set our sights on California, we'd keep pushing harder."

And that's what they did. The Mariners began making a habit of coming from behind to win. They would do it twelve times in September alone.

"We went into every game at home anticipating some kind of miracle or something," said Randy Johnson. "For the most part, something miraculous *did* happen."

Starting on September 18, the Mariners embarked on a seven-game win streak against Texas, Oakland, and California. When they won on September 21, they pulled even with the Angels. Seattle had made up 13 games between August 2 and September 21. The next night, when they came from behind again to beat Oakland 10–7, the team moved into sole possession of first place in the American League West. The Mariners had won 22 of 29 games and were the talk of the town.

"We've used different weapons," said Manager Piniella. "With Junior out, we've created our own identity. We didn't have to rely on one person. If you told me in spring training that we would have four players with a shot at knocking in 100 runs—and one of them wouldn't be Junior—I'd have looked at you funny."

But that's what was happening. Buhner, Edgar and Tino Martinez, and Mike Blowers all had a shot at 100 ribbys. As for Junior, he continued to struggle somewhat after his return. His batting average at one point was under .250 as he tried to get his exquisite sense of timing back. But as long as the team was winning, he was willing to take the trade-off.

During the seven-game win streak in September, Junior finally got hot. He batted .448, getting 13 hits in 29 at-bats. He also had four homers and 12 RBIs in the seven games, including at least one ribby in each contest. And, as Lou Piniella said, he didn't have to take so much responsibility on his shoulders. The other players had matured and were delivering in the clutch, as well.

On September 28, Junior blasted the eighth grand-slam homer of his career as the Mariners beat Texas, 6–2, to maintain their lead. But to the Angels' credit, they didn't quit, either. When the regular season ended, the two teams were tied with identical 78–66 records. They had to meet in a one-game playoff for the A.L. West crown. The irony was that the Yankees had finished with a 79–65 record in the A.L. East. They would be the wild card team. The loser of the playoff between the Mariners and Angels would be going home. So everything was at stake.

There were more ironies. The pitching matchup had big Randy Johnson going for the Mariners against the Angels' Mark Langston. Langston had started his career as a Mariner and was traded to the Montreal Expos in May 1989. One of the players coming to Seattle in the deal was Randy Johnson. Now the two would meet in the biggest game of their respective careers.

It stayed close for six innings. Johnson was throwing smoke and was perfect for five and two-thirds innings before the Angels got their first hit. Still, the Mariners held a 1–0 lead going into the bottom of the seventh. With 52,356 fans urging them on, Seattle finally broke it open. The big hit was a bases-loaded double by infielder Luis Sojo, who also scored when Langston made a throwing error. As usual, everyone contributed. From there, the Mariners went on to win it 9–1, with Johnson throwing a three-hitter and striking out 12.

The Mariners had done it! They were division champs and would be making their first trip to the postseason in the nineteen-year history of the franchise. The players were ecstatic.

"I felt a little bit of weight on my shoulders," Johnson said. "But I thrive on that and it was probably my biggest game ever. I had a lot of emotion built up."

Junior, for one, recognized that the team's ace hurler had that little extra special thing going.

"When he stepped on the field today . . . there was something about him," Junior said. "It was like, 'Give me one run and I'll take care of the rest.'"

Unlike seasons past, the big numbers in the regular season did not belong exclusively to Junior. Edgar Martinez won his second American League batting championship with a .356 average, tied for the league lead with 52 doubles, clubbed 29 homers, and drove home 113 runs. He had, simply, a super season. Jay Buhner finally emerged as one of the league's top sluggers, with career bests 40 home runs and 121 RBIs.

Tino Martinez also had his best year, hitting .293 with 31 home runs and 111 runs batted in. Third sacker Mike Blowers clubbed 23 homers and just missed the 100-RBI mark with 96.

On the mound, Randy Johnson was incredible. He finished with an 18–2 record. The Big Unit led the league with a 2.48 earned run average and 294 strikeouts. The other starters were spotty, though Andy Benes was 7–2 after joining the team at the end of July. The bullpen trio of Bobby Ayala, Jeff Nelson, and Norm Charlton had 35 saves between them.

As for Junior, his overall season had been pretty much affected by the broken wrist. He wound up hitting a career-low .258, with 17 homers and 42 RBIs in 260 at-bats. Despite his injury, he still won another Gold Glove, and had also been voted a starter in the All-Star Game, though the fans had known he couldn't play. With the playoffs now looming dead ahead, Junior was about to show the baseball world that his regular-season numbers didn't really count. He was still one of baseball's best.

It was the first year of the extended playoffs, with four teams in each league having a chance at the World Series. As Western Division champs, the Mariners would have to play the wild card team in the first-round best-of-five series. And that wild card team was the New York Yankees.

The Yanks and Mariners already had quite a rivalry. It began with Manager Piniella, who had been a player for the Yanks when the Bronx Bombers won back-to-back World Series in 1977 and 1978. He also managed the Yanks for three years and won a World Series as manager of the Cincinnati Reds in 1990. So he knew what the postseason was all about. There was also a feeling among the Mariners that they could handle the Yanks at the Kingdome. But the first two games of the series would be played at Yankee Stadium. And because Randy Johnson had to pitch against the Angels in the one-game playoff, he wouldn't be ready to go against the Yanks until game three. So it wouldn't be an easy road.

Game one had Yankee ace David Cone facing the Mariners' Chris Bosio, who was just 10–8 on the season. The game stayed scoreless until the Yanks tallied a pair in the bottom of the third. Junior then led off the fourth for the Mariners. Cone worked the count to 1-2, then tried a splitter. Showing no ill effects of the wrist injury, Junior turned on it and sent a shot down the right field line and into the seats. Home run! The lead was now 2–1.

Seattle tied the game in the sixth, but the Yanks took a 4–2 lead into the seventh. After Joey Cora drew a one-out walk, Junior came up again. This time he went after Cone's first pitch and drilled it high and deep into the right field stands, his second home run of the game. More importantly, it tied matters at 4–4. But the Seattle bullpen couldn't do the job. The Yanks broke it open with four in the seventh and went on to take a 9–6 victory.

It had been a great playoff debut for Junior, who added a single and run scored in the ninth. But it wasn't enough. Now Seattle had to hope Andy Benes could get them even in game two. The veteran righty would be opposed by Yankees rookie left-hander Andy Pettitte. It turned out to be a game for the ages.

The game would go 15 innings and take five hours and twelve minutes to play, the longest postseason game ever. It was tied at 4–4 at the end of nine. In the top of the twelfth, Junior came up again. Facing Yankee relief ace John Wetteland, he jacked another one, a long shot into the right center field seats. It was his third homer in two days and gave the Mariners a 5–4 lead. Unfortunately, the Yanks tied it in their half of the inning, then won it on a Jim Leyritz two-run homer in the fifteenth. Despite the heroics of Ken Griffey, Jr., the Mariners would be returning to Seattle down 2–0, and just one game away from elimination.

But once again Randy Johnson came to the rescue. The Big Unit gave up just two runs in seven innings in game three, striking out 10, and besting veteran Jack McDowell. Johnson left with a 6–2 lead and the Mariners went on to win the game, 7–4. Tino Martinez was the batting hero with three hits and three RBIs. Now came game four, with Chris Bosio taking the hill for Seattle against the Yanks' Scott Kamieniecki. This one really had the 57,180 fans in the Kingdome climbing the wall.

It looked bleak when the Yanks drove Bosio to the showers by taking a 5–0 lead by the top of the third inning. But this was a Mariners team that now knew how to come from behind. They wasted no time. In the bottom of the third, Edgar Martinez hit a three-run shot and the Mariners added another to cut the lead to 5–4. Then they tied the game in the bottom of the fifth.

With the score still tied in the bottom of the sixth, Junior came up against lefty reliever Sterling Hitchcock. As with all great hitters, when he's in the zone, lefty or righty doesn't matter to him. It was just a matter of seeing the ball and hitting it. He promptly picked out a Hitchcock fastball and drove it into the seats to give the Mariners a 6–5 lead. It was his fourth homer of the series, a new record for the playoffs.

The Yanks tied the game in the top of the eighth, but Seattle settled things quickly in the bottom of the inning. Edgar Martinez did the bulk of the damage with a grand-slam homer off John Wetteland, giving him a record seven RBIs for the game. Jay Buhner followed with a dinger off Steve Howe and the Mariners went on to win, 11–8, to tie the series, setting up a fifth and decisive game.

With Randy Johnson not available, the Mariners turned to Andy Benes to pitch the fifth game. The Yanks countered with their top pitcher, David Cone. This would be a game that Seattle fans would remember for a long time. It started as if it would be a pitchers' battle. The game was still scoreless when the Mariners came to bat in the bottom of the third and got the long ball from a surprising source. Second sacker Joey Cora, who had hit only three homers all year, took David Cone deep on a 1-0 pitch. His solo shot gave the Mariners the early lead.

The Yanks came right back in the fourth, taking the lead on the two-run homer by Paul O'Neill, but Seattle tied it at two-all in their half of the inning on a Tino Martinez double and a single by Buhner. But then in the top of the sixth the Yanks took the lead again, getting a pair of runs for a 4–2 advantage. And time was getting short.

When Cora flied out to start the Seattle eighth, the Mariners had just five outs left. Now Junior was up once more, facing Cone. With the count at 1-0, he did it again. Picking on a Cone fastball, Junior stroked yet another long home run to right field. It was his fifth homer in five playoff games, and it closed the gap to 4–3. Before the inning ended, the Mariners had tied the game on a bases-loaded walk. Then, in the ninth, Seattle gambled by bringing Randy Johnson into the game on just a day's rest.

Tired as he was, the Big Unit set the Yanks down in the ninth. But when the Mariners couldn't score off Jack McDowell, making the first relief appearance of his career, the game went into extra innings.

In the top of the eleventh, the Yanks broke through, Randy Velarde singling home the go-ahead run off the fatigued Johnson. Now the Mariners were down 5–4, and also down to their last three outs. Would they be the last three outs of the season?

Joey Cora was up first and dropped down a perfect bunt. Base hit. Now Junior strode to the plate and the Kingdome erupted in a huge roar. Could he belt another one, a sixth homer? McDowell worked carefully, but Junior slammed a solid single to center, Cora racing around to third. Now the red-hot Edgar Martinez was up. The Yanks stayed with McDowell. Martinez went after a high fastball and slammed the ball down the left field line into the corner. Cora scored easily. Now all eyes were on Junior.

He raced around second and really turned on the speed. When the ball momentarily eluded left fielder Gerald Williams, Coach Sam Perlozzo—who later said Griffey was "running faster than I've ever seen him before"—waved Junior home. The throw came to shortstop Tony Fernandez, who whirled and fired toward the plate. Junior slid across the dish in a cloud of dust. He was safe! The Mariners had won it, taking three straight after being down 2–0.

The fans in the Kingdome were in a frenzy, waving REFUSE TO LOSE banners and T-shirts. The Seattle dugout emptied and players mobbed Junior, whose speed and hustle resulted in the winning run.

"All the hard work we did finally paid off for us," a jubilant Griffey said afterward.

He had come all the way back from the broken wrist that had sabotaged his season. Despite the metal plate and screws still in his wrist, he had belted a record five homers in five games, getting nine total hits in the series, batting .391, and driving in seven runs. In fact, Griffey and Edgar Martinez, hitting third and fourth in the Seattle lineup, combined for a .477 average, seven home runs, and 17 RBIs. They were a two-man wrecking crew.

But it wasn't over yet. Now the Mariners had to meet the Cleveland Indians in a best-of-seven American League Championship Series. The winner would go to the World Series.

The Indians were led by speedy Kenny Lofton, and sluggers Albert Belle, Jim Thome, Manny Ramirez, and Sandy Alomar, Jr. They also had a pair of seasoned veteran pitchers in Dennis Martinez and Orel Hershiser, as well as a top closer in Jose Mesa. During the regular season Cleveland had the best record in baseball (100–44), winning the American League Central Division by an amazing 30 games. They would not be an easy team to beat.

With the pitching staff tired, Manager Piniella tabbed rookie Bob Wolcott to start the opener in the Kingdome. It looked like the Mariners had pulled a rabbit out of the hat. Wolcott gave them seven solid innings and Seattle won the opener 3–2, Luis Sojo knocking in the winning run in the seventh inning. Junior continued his hot hitting with a single and a double in three trips.

Cleveland got even the next night as veteran Orel Hershiser bested veteran Tim Belcher, 5–2. The only bright spot for the Mariners was the sixth postseason home run for Ken Griffey, Jr. Though he gladly would have traded the dinger for a victory, Junior became the first American League player ever to hit six home runs in the postseason.

Now the scene shifted to Cleveland, where Randy Johnson took the mound against the Indians' Charles Nagy. This was a close one, tied at 2–2 after nine. The Mariners won it when Jay Buhner slammed a three-run homer in the eleventh inning. Norm Charlton, with three scoreless innings of relief, got the victory. Junior had two more hits, stole a base, and scored a run in the win.

With a chance to take a commanding 3–1 lead, the Mariners ran into a hot pitcher. Cleveland's Ken Hill threw seven scoreless innings as the Indians raked Andy Benes early and won it, 7–0. The series was tied at two games each, and for just the second time in the playoffs, Junior went hitless. Now came the pivotal fifth game, with Chris Bosio going up against the veteran Hershiser.

This was a close one. Cleveland got a run in the first, but the Mariners tied it in the third, then went ahead in the fifth, with Junior doubling home the second run. It stayed that way until the bottom of the sixth, when Cleveland's Jim Thome slammed a two-run homer off Bosio to give the Indians a 3–2 lead. And that's the way it ended. Now the Mariners returned to the Kingdome and were one game from elimination. But they had also won 20 of their last 24 games in their noisy building. So there was still hope.

Manager Piniella called upon a tired Randy Johnson to face Cleveland's Dennis Martinez. It would be the fourth time the Big Unit took to the mound in the last 15 days. But the Mariners had the amazing record of 30–3 when Johnson pitched in 1995. They all hoped he could do it one more time.

The game was scoreless for four. Then, in the top of the fifth, the Indians broke through after a two-base throwing error by Joey Cora. Kenny Lofton followed with a single, giving the Tribe a 1–0 lead. It stayed that way until the eighth, when the tired Johnson finally faltered. The Indians pushed across three runs to take a 4–0 lead. Johnson left to a standing ovation, and a short time later the entire Mariners team got an ovation, a thank-you for a great season which had finally ended.

Dennis Martinez and two relievers four-hit the Mariners to end their magical season. The 4–0 score held up and it was the Indians that moved on to the World Series.

"We hung in as long as we could," Junior said afterward. "We just picked the wrong time to stop hitting."

That was certainly true. After batting .315 as a team against the Yanks, the M's hit just .184 collectively against the Indians. Junior still managed a .333 average, but had only one homer and two ribbys to show for his seven hits. Edgar Martinez, who flailed away at an incredible .571 clip against the Yanks, hit an anemic .087 (2 for 23) in the ALCS. Tino Martinez had a .136 average, Vince Coleman batted .100, Joey Cora .174, and catcher Dan Wilson failed to get a single hit in 16 at-bats.

But no one could fault the Mariners. They had

finally arrived, made a great stretch run to catch the Angels, then defeated the mighty Yanks in a heart-stopping opening round. The only irony to the season was that the Mariners had their greatest year while their greatest player had his poorest season.

It was the broken wrist that had set Ken Griffey, Jr., back. In the playoffs against the Yanks, he showed all over again the kind of force he could be. He was still only twenty-five years old at the end of the 1995 season. Yet he had already been in the big leagues for seven full seasons. There was every reason to believe the best was still to come.

And some of the best came just four days after the Mariners were eliminated by the Indians. That's when Melissa Griffey gave birth to the couple's second child, a daughter they named Taryn Kennedy Griffey. Junior's family was growing, and so was his fame.

Chapter 11

Junior and the Seattle Sluggers

On December 3, Junior had another grim reminder of the injury that helped derail his 1995 season. He underwent surgery to have the metal plate and seven surgical screws removed from his left wrist. The fact that he was able to hit six postseason home runs must have made him seem like something of a bionic man. He hoped the wrist would be all the way back in 1996 and he could again have a full season of good health.

In 1994 there was talk of him breaking Roger Maris's single-season home run record of 61. But that year ended in mid-August thanks to the Players' Association strike. The next year it was the wrist. But at least he was able to come back and help the Mariners win their division. The Mariners and their fans hoped it would all come together in 1996 for both Junior and the team.

The 1995 season had created something else that would continue into the new season: Mariner mania. The team had been given new life in Seattle and for the first time there was citywide interest in the REFUSE TO LOSE Mariners. Junior and his teammates were all looked upon as heroes. In fact, the city of Seattle seemed to realize it had a real national treasure in Ken Griffey, Jr.

By this time, whenever someone started a debate about the best all-around player in the game, only two names would generally be mentioned. One was Barry Bonds, the three-time Most Valuable Player who was now with the San Francisco Giants. The other was Ken Griffey, Jr. Both hit for average, hit for power, were Gold Glove outfielders, could run and throw. The only difference was age. Junior would be just twenty-six at the start of the 1996 season. Bonds was just four months from his thirty-second birthday. Bonds was already the best he could be. Junior was still getting better. And he would prove that again during the upcoming season.

There had been a few changes in the Mariners team. Slugging first baseman Tino Martinez had signed a free-agent contract with the New York Yankees. And a trade with the Yankees had seen valuable reliever Jeff Nelson and utility infielder Luis Sojo depart. Left-handed starter Sterling Hitchcock and third base prospect Russ Davis came over to Seattle. Paul Sorrento, another hard-hitting first baseman, was signed to replace Martinez.

The other major change was the team's new

shortstop. Manager Piniella had handed the job to twenty-year-old Alex Rodriguez. The youngster had played 48 games at short the year before and hit just .232, with five homers in 142 at-bats. But the feeling was that Rodriguez had the potential to be a star and would be given a full shot at the job. Absolutely no one could have predicted what he would do.

As was the case the year before, the only real question mark was pitching. Beyond Randy Johnson, there were no proven starters and the bullpen was considered iffy at best. Except when the Big Unit was on the mound, the Mariners might have to hit their way to victory. And that was something they seemed prepared to do.

The Mariners won their opener against the White Sox 3–2 in 11 innings. Johnson went seven innings and fanned 14 hitters. While he didn't get the decision, he seemed more dominating than ever. The club won their first two, then lost two, then won a pair, and subsequently lost a pair. So they were 4–4 when they embarked on an eight-game winning streak that ran their record to 12–4 and saw them take over first place in the A.L. West.

Johnson won three games during the streak and just about everyone was hitting. Shortstop Rodriguez was a real surprise. Not only was he playing outstanding ball in the field, but he was hitting like a demon, showing power no one knew he had and sporting an average well over .300. As for Junior, he got off to a slow start averagewise, but there was little doubt that all his power had returned . . . and maybe more.

On April 12 in Toronto, the second game of the eight-game win streak, he blasted a pair of home runs, his fourth and fifth of the year. The second one was a real moon shot. The ball traveled into the deck above the Hard Rock Café, located high in the right field stands at SkyDome. He never ceased to amaze with a sudden explosion of his bat.

In fact, according to former teammate Tino Martinez, Junior had become a much more accomplished hitter than when he had first arrived on the scene.

"Early in his career we'd go over scouting reports on pitchers, and Junior wouldn't bother listening," Martinez said. "He didn't care who was throwing or what the guy threw. He just looked for the ball and hit it. A lot of pitchers were trying to figure him out, so they would challenge him—see if he could hit a good inside fastball, see what he did with breaking balls. They tried to find weaknesses. Obviously, there were none.

"Now he's hitting with all the knowledge that comes from experience. I see him setting up pitchers all the time, which you didn't see earlier. He might look bad on a certain pitch, and when a pitcher comes back with the same pitch, maybe in the next at-bat or with two strikes, he'll be sitting on it and crush it."

There was little doubt that Junior was still improving, still getting better. And with the support he was getting from Edgar Martinez, Buhner, and young Alex Rodriguez, the Mariners had a modern-day version of Murderers' Row, the nickname given the slugging 1927 Yankees. Early on it was looking as if the team had a great chance to repeat as division champs and return to the play-offs for a second straight year.

That's when the unthinkable happened. With a 4–0 record in five starts, Randy Johnson was taking up just where he had left off the year before, leading the league in strikeouts and dominating hitters. On April 26, he made his next scheduled start at Milwaukee. But after just three and two-thirds innings, the Big Unit suddenly took himself out of the game. He was suffering from severe lower back pain.

He made his next start on May 1 at Texas, and this time could pitch only two innings. The back pain forced him to the sidelines once more. On May 12 at Kansas City, he tried it again. This time he lasted five-plus innings and actually got his fifth win. But again back pain left him unable to go any further. Seattle's team doctors gave him a thorough examination. The news wasn't good. The Big Unit was suffering from an irritated nerve in his lower back. The team had to put him on the disabled list. He wouldn't make another start all year.

Johnson was probably the player the Mariners could least afford to lose. As great as Junior was, there were some very solid hitters behind him. The Big Unit was not only the team's ace, but its only really reliable starter and big winner. The ball club was already pitching-thin. Without Johnson, the rest of the season would be a struggle.

In early August, Johnson would try it again, making several brief relief appearances. He still had the ability to strike batters out, but once again the pain returned. By August 27, he was back on the disabled list and on September 12 underwent surgery to correct an extruded disk herniation in his lower back. All the Mariners could hope for was that he could return to full strength in 1997.

So the team carried on, hitting perhaps like no other team in the league. It was a year in which many experts felt the ball was "juiced." It seemed to be carrying farther, and former Punch and Judy hitters were suddenly reaching the seats with regularity.

A random sampling of scores from 1996 shows how the Mariners hit and how poorly they often pitched. During the year they would win games by scores of 11–10, 16–10, 13–7, 9–8, 13–12, 18–8, 19–8, and 15–3. Conversely, they lost games of 16–7, 16–9, 14–13, 12–8, 11–6, 9–8, 10–5, and 13–11. So while they were more than capable of scoring runs in bunches, they were also capable of giving them up in bunches.

Unfortunately, Junior and the other big hitters couldn't pitch, too. They could only do their thing to the maximum and hope for the best. Early on, Junior established a new team record by clubbing eight homers in the month of April. Then, on May 21, he hit the 200th home run of his career off Vaughn Eshelman of the Red Sox, becoming the seventh youngest player in history to reach that milestone.

He was twenty-six years 181 days old when he connected. The youngest was Mel Ott, who was twenty-five years 144 days when he hit his 200th.

The others in between were Eddie Mathews, Jimmie Foxx, Mickey Mantle, Frank Robinson, and Henry Aaron. That's quite a list. All six are in the Hall of Fame. Aaron wound up with 755, the most in history. Of the others, Ott had the fewest, finishing with 511 dingers. And since Junior seemed to be hitting with more power as the years passed, there was still no telling how high on the list he might go.

Most of the other home run sluggers were big, muscular players—like Mark McGwire, Frank Thomas, and Albert Belle. And in an age of advanced methods of training, many of them worked out regularly, pumping iron or using strength machines to be able to hit the ball farther. Junior was almost a throwback to the earlier days, when players did it naturally. One observer called him "a low-maintenance hitter." And Tino Martinez remarked that he had "a perfect swing, something that can't be taught."

He also rarely used videotape to analyze his hitting style and correct flaws. If he did, it was just to check out the position of his hands at the beginning of his swing. Yet he still hit the ball every bit as far as the so-called big boppers who had size and muscles on top of muscles. But Junior felt the key was in a single word.

"Flexibility," he said. "Just look at Tiger Woods."

Tiger Woods, of course, was the young golfing sensation who could drive a ball more than 300 yards off the tee with regularity. Yet he weighed a mere 165 pounds. Those analyzing Woods's golf swing would say that it was flexibility and quickness that generated the power. Well, it was the same for Ken Griffey, Jr.

In mid-May, Junior started on one of his patented hitting tears. From May 15 to 25, he batted .488, getting 21 hits in 43 at-bats. And on May 24 against the archrival Yankees, he had one of the best days of his career. Not only did he go a perfect four-for-four, raising his batting average above .300 for the first time all season, but he also had the first three-homer game of his career. Not surprisingly, he was named American League Player of the Week.

By the end of May, the Mariners had a 28–24 record and trailed the division-leading Texas Rangers by five and a half games. It was already apparent that the team missed Randy Johnson terribly. But they were still a ball club that no opposing pitcher looked forward to facing. Junior, Jay Buhner, and Edgar Martinez were all on a pace to equal or surpass their best seasons. But the big surprise continued to be young Alex Rodriguez. He was up among the leaders in hitting and several other offensive categories. These Mariners were a lumber company to be reckoned with every game.

By mid-June, the Mariners were 35–30 and still five games behind Texas. Junior, however, was having a great year, up among the leaders in both home runs and RBIs. When he stepped to the plate for his first at-bat in a game against Toronto on June 19, he already had 23 home runs and 61 RBIs in just 67 games. With 95 games remaining, he was a good bet to top 50 homers and maybe go over the

150-RBI mark. That's the kind of year he was having.

But then Lady Luck stepped in once more. In his first at-bat against the Blue Jays, he felt a sharp pain in his right wrist and had to leave the game. X rays showed that a small bone, called the hamate bone, had broken. The next day he had surgery to remove the bone and was placed on the 15-day disabled list. Though the injury wasn't as serious as the one in 1995, it marked the second straight season that Junior had been derailed by a wrist injury.

While Junior was recuperating, Manager Piniella and others suggested he temper his style a bit, think twice about diving for the ball in the outfield or going for catches against the wall. Junior didn't want to hear that.

"Whatever I'm going to do, I'm going to do," he said. "I don't feel I'll be more cautious. If that were the case, then I might as well be a designated hitter."

During his stint on the DL, Junior learned that he was once again the top vote-getter for the All-Star Game. This time he garnered 3,064,814 votes. It marked the seventh straight year he had been voted an All-Star starter by the fans. Unfortunately, it was also the second straight year he missed the game because of an injury. That was one streak he didn't want to continue. Finally, after missing 20 games, he was ready to return to action. That came on July 14, in a game at the Kingdome against the California Angels.

Judging by Junior's performance, it looked as if

he had never been away. He slammed a double and his twenty-fourth home run in five trips to the plate. In his absence, the Mariners had been 12–8 and were now 49–40, three games behind Texas. They still had a chance to win the division. So once again Junior began playing with his usual all-out style. But while it may have appeared to the fans as if Junior was all the way back, as was the case the year before, it wasn't easy for him.

"People don't realize what I deal with on a day-to-day basis," he said. "I break both wrists, and when I go back out there, it's supposed to be like I never was hurt."

Junior would reveal later that he played his first six weeks back without any feeling in his right pinky and ring finger as the result of the broken bone and subsequent surgery. But he said it was even worse in 1995. When he returned from the more serious break of his left wrist, the worst thing he could do was swing at a pitch and miss. When that happened, he felt a sharp pain shoot up from his left wrist into his arm.

"It felt as if somebody were pulling my arm out from the wrist," he said.

But like all great athletes, Junior was a gamer. He played and played well, mostly without complaint. The team came first and he was determined to do everything he could to help them win and return to the playoffs. He played the second half of the season in a wonderful groove, once again showing he was one of the very top power hitters in the game, and its best center fielder.

Unfortunately, without Randy Johnson and some strong pitching behind him, the Mariners fell short. They finished the season with an 85–76 record. That was the most wins in franchise history (remember, the 1995 season was shortened to 144 games), but it still left them four and a half games behind division-winning Texas. Worse yet, they were two and a half games behind Baltimore in the race for the wild card. So there would be no postseason in 1996. It was a real shame. For the Mariners' hitters had otherwise produced a truly memorable season, fully appreciated by the record 2,723,850 fans who came to the Kingdome, over a half million more than had ever come before in a single season.

As a team, the Mariners hit .287, fourth best in the league. And they led all American League teams in runs scored, total bases, doubles, and runs batted in. Their 245 team home runs broke the old record of 240 set by the 1961 New York Yankees, but was second to the Orioles' 257. For overall run production, however, the Mariners were tops.

Much of the damage was done by six players. Edgar Martinez hit .327, with 52 doubles, 26 homers, and 103 runs batted in. Jay Buhner had his best year ever, slamming 44 home runs and driving in 138 runs. Paul Sorrento had 23 homers and 93 ribbys, while catcher Dan Wilson hit 18 dingers and drove home 83 runs.

Young Alex Rodriguez emerged as a full-fledged star with a truly incredible season. He led the

American League in hitting with a .358 average, clubbed 36 home runs, and drove home 123 runs. He also led the league with 141 runs scored, 379 total bases, and 54 doubles. He was the third-youngest-ever American League batting champ, was second to Juan Gonzalez of Texas in the Most Valuable Player voting, and was named Associated Press Player of the Year. At age twenty-one, his future seemed limitless.

And so did Junior's. Despite missing 20 games with the broken wrist, he had still produced his best season. Playing in 140 games, Junior hit .303, slammed 49 big home runs, and drove home 140 runs. In fact, he became just the ninth player in baseball since 1940 to have driven home a run per game. Had he not sat out those 20 games with the broken wrist, he certainly would have cracked the 50-home-run barrier and probably would have driven home more than 150 runs. Chances are he would have led the league in both categories. Big Mark McGwire led with 52 homers, while Cleveland's Albert Belle was the top RBI man with 148.

But don't mention those numbers to Junior. Milestones are great, something to be looked back upon and cherished once your career is over. The here and now, however, was about winning.

"People don't understand," he reiterated, referring to the attention given numbers, statistics, and records. "I'm not a record guy. I don't pay attention to that. . . . My thing is if I can win a championship. My dad has three of them. I'd like to end my career with one.

"When you talk about players and dynasties, people always bring up the '75–'76 Reds. No matter what happens, these guys we'll remember forever—not one player, but the whole team. That's how I want to be remembered—as someone who played on a team that won."

Chapter 12

How Much Better
Can He Get?

The prolonged players' strike in 1994 had taken a big chunk out of baseball's popularity. Since that time, the sport seemed to be regaining some of its lost luster. But there were still criticisms, mainly that baseball could no longer call itself the national pastime. And the most common reason given was that the sport was losing its young fans. Kids were more interested in playing sports like soccer and basketball, and watching athletes like Michael Jordan, Shaquille O'Neal, and Grant Hill, all major basketball stars.

Why weren't the kids as interested in baseball in 1997? Part of it might be the proliferation of night games. There was a time when the All-Star Game, the World Series, and weekend games were almost always played in the afternoon. Kids could watch their favorite players then, even spend more time at

the ballpark. They had memories of the big events—
a dramatic home run, a great catch, the joyous
celebration after a big win—that they carried into
adulthood. Thus, they remained fans forever.

Now, with these games often starting at 8 or 8:30
P.M. and not ending until nearly midnight, many of
these young fans are out of touch, in bed much too
early to see the great performances that were once
etched firmly in the memories of young fans, who
then became lifelong followers of the game.

Then there were the players. Many of them
seemed to have become surly and unfriendly,
especially the superstars. Some just gave the im-
pression that they didn't need the fans anymore.
They knew they were going to sign multimillion-
dollar contracts whether they were fan favorites or
not. Others were simply overwhelmed by the endless questions of the media, by people swarming
them for autographs or a handshake, and perhaps
by the feeling that there are too many crazies in
the world, people looking to make a name by
harming a celebrity.

There is some truth to all of this, but in fact, if
baseball wants to bring back its young fans, it has
to start with the players. And as of 1997, the player
considered baseball's best ambassador to the
young fan was Ken Griffey, Jr. As one writer put it,
"Ken Griffey, Jr., represents baseball's last hope. It
goes beyond home runs and history. It's about a
friendly nod, a wink or wave, simple courtesy and
kindness. . . . This is what separates Griffey [from
other superstars], what makes him seem human in

an elitist world, what makes him the best candidate for baseball's savior."

That's a pretty heavy load to put on the shoulders of one man. But it's a sentiment echoed by players and fans alike.

"He's good people," said Mariners backup catcher John Marzano. "I've seen him spend two hours before a game taking kids in wheelchairs around, showing them his locker, signing stuff for them, hanging out like they're old friends."

Former teammate Tino Martinez didn't mince words when he said, "He's the best player in the game, and he relates to the fans and the kids better than anyone."

This was confirmed by a fourteen-year-old from Detroit who waited to see Junior every time the Mariners came to town.

"If the Kid [Junior] wasn't here, we wouldn't be here," the youngster said. "He's just nice. He's always having fun. He plays with the crowd. He says 'hi' to us. Everyone else, they're just like all business. He's more childlike. He's like us."

Junior himself admitted that he often had a special feeling for the fans and didn't want to lose it.

"I really like the fans," he said. "I try to sign [autographs] as often as I can. They make signs for me. Things like that, you appreciate. It makes you feel good. When people go out of their way to do things for me, I go out of my way to do things for them.

"That's just the way I am. I'm not a guy who just takes. You know, I really don't want anything. . . . I just try to treat people like people."

Junior gave in other ways, as well. In 1994 he received the Celebrity Recognition Award from the Make-A-Wish Foundation and the A. Bartlett Giamatti Award from the Baseball Assistance Team (BAT) in recognition of his "caring for fellow citizens." And since December of 1994 he has sponsored Christmas dinners for 350 youngsters from the Rainier Vista Boys and Girls Club.

Then on January 31, 1996, he announced the beginning of the "Junior's Kids Center" program, which provides tickets for underprivileged kids to attend all the Mariners' Saturday night games. For these efforts and others, he was selected as the 1996 Mariners' Roberto Clemente Award winner for outstanding community service.

So Junior already had a special place in the game when the 1997 season got under way. His primary goal at the outset of the new season was to stay healthy. He hadn't played a full season uninterrupted by strike or injury since 1993. That year he belted 45 homers at the age of twenty-three. He had already heard the predictions that a healthy Griffey could break Roger Maris's home run record. He had heard that before and his answer was always basically the same. In 1997, he put it this way: "You never heard those expectations come from me, the 61 home runs, the 150 RBIs. I just go out and play hard, and whatever happens, happens."

What he also hoped would happen was a return to the playoffs for the Mariners. The cast of characters was basically the same. There was no reason to believe the M's wouldn't be the most feared hitting team in the league once more. The question remained the pitching. Randy Johnson was returning from back surgery and the ball club could only hope he was the Big Unit of old, which meant the most intimidating pitcher in the league. The team also signed two more veteran starters, lefties Jeff Fassero and Jamie Moyer. If they pitched to their potential the team would have three solid starters. The bullpen was still questionable, and Manager Piniella hoped a reliable closer would emerge between veterans Norm Charlton and Bobby Ayala.

But once the season started, the story in Seattle returned to a familiar theme. Johnson was pitching well again, the hitters were hitting, and the team was winning. But the biggest story of them all was Junior. He started out as if he wanted to cram a full season into the first month. A year earlier, he had set a club record with eight homers in April. This year he looked as if he was after much more.

The ball was jumping off his bat and more often than not landing somewhere over the outfield fences. Despite the wrist injuries of the past two seasons, everyone began to feel that Junior was not only all the way back, he was even better than before. He already held the record for the most home runs by the end of May (22) and by the end of June (32), both set in 1994 when his season was stopped by the strike.

Now he seemed to have a bead on the mark for April. The record was 11, shared by contemporaries Barry Bonds, Gary Sheffield, and Brady Anderson, as well as former sluggers Willie Stargell, Graig Nettles, and Mike Schmidt. It was a crowded field. When Junior took to the diamond to face the Toronto Blue Jays at SkyDome on Friday night, April 25, he already had 10 homers in April. But on this night he would be facing Jays' righty Roger Clemens, who came into the game with a microscopic 0.46 earned run average.

Then early in the game Junior showed he was zeroed in. He picked out a Clemens fastball and drove it into the right field seats. It was his eleventh home run of the month, putting him into the record book with the six other players. He didn't stop there, however. He was about to not only remove his fellow players from the book, but reach another milestone, as well.

It happened when he came up in the seventh inning. Clemens was still on the mound. Junior waited in his familiar stance, bat held high over his left shoulder, feet close together. Clemens threw the fastball again, the same heater that had overmatched so many hitters over the years. Not Junior. Not this time. Once again his picture-perfect swing was right on the money. The ball jumped off the bat like it had been shot out of a cannon. And when it landed, Junior was again circling the bases in his home run trot.

It was his twelfth homer in April, a new major league mark. In addition, it was the 250th home run of his career. That was a mark only three players in history had reached at a younger age than Griffey. They were Jimmie Foxx, Eddie Mathews, and Mel Ott. When Junior had reached the 200 homer mark, there were six players who had reached it at an earlier age. At the 250 mark there were three. Junior's homer frequency was advancing him in the record books.

He still wasn't finished for the night, however. The hard-hitting Mariners had sent Clemens to the showers, and when Junior came up again in the eighth inning, relief pitcher Mike Timlin was on the mound. Once again Junior unleashed his bat, and once again the ball left the yard. It was his thirteenth home run of the month, extending the record he had set earlier in the night. It was also his third career three-homer game and it extended the Seattle lead to 13–7. It also gave him 30 RBIs on the season.

When asked about the record and the milestone he had reached, Junior, as always, kept it simple. "I know where the barrel of my bat is at all times," he said. "All my life I've known what pitches I can and cannot hit."

His great April helped move the Mariners into first place in the American League West and it once again brought up talk about the Roger Maris home run record, set back in 1961.

"If he stays healthy, he'll get it easily," said former teammate Jeff Nelson, who was now with the Yankees. "He has power to all fields. He hits all pitchers and he's not fooled very often. And on top of that, he doesn't care about pressure."

One writer agreed with that last assessment. "Next to his swing, his competitive nature, and his touch for the clutch, Griffey's loosey-goosey personality will be his greatest ally. Unlike [some of the other top sluggers], Griffey doesn't tense up at mention of the record. He doesn't clench his teeth at the sight of a media mob heading his way. He knows what it will take to break Maris's record and he's not afraid to talk about it. How refreshing."

Though he talked about it, as usual he kept it simple. Though he still insisted he didn't focus on records, he did know what it would take and expressed it in very basic terms.

"Number one, you've got to stay healthy," Junior said. "Number two, you've got to be pitched to. Number three, you've got to stay consistent the whole season."

All three points were well taken. Injuries had hurt Junior the last two seasons. As far as being pitched to, Junior was lucky in that respect. He had such outstanding hitters around him in the lineup that opposing teams wouldn't be inclined to work around him, to give him bad pitches, or walk him intentionally. With Alex Rodriguez, Edgar Martinez, and Jay Buhner to protect him in the lineup, Junior would get his share of good pitches to hit.

Consistency was the third point. To break the home run record, he couldn't afford to have any long droughts when he didn't hit homers or hit just a few. So breaking the record was easier said than done.

One reason most people felt Junior had the best chance was a quick look at his last 162 games, the equivalent of a full season. Someone pointed out that by taking the 140 games Junior played in 1996 and the first 22 games of 1997, his numbers for those 162 games read thusly—a .313 batting average, 170 runs batted in, and 62 home runs. It's still not known whether Junior will ever put a season like that together, but he is certainly capable of doing it.

Manager Piniella also saw Junior's great potential, but felt he was such a confident hitter that he often went after pitches that were out of the strike zone.

"When Junior makes the pitcher put the ball over the plate, he's going to get a good swing at it," Lou said. "That's what he's been doing more and more [this year]. The problem in the past was that Junior saw the ball so well he felt as if he could hit everything they threw. I tell him, 'If they want to walk you, let them walk you. You're capable of winning the Triple Crown.'"

By the end of April, the Mariners were once again the hardest-hitting team in the majors. They were scoring at a 6.1-runs-per-game clip, very close to the 1996 version of the team. And that was the highest-scoring team in forty-six years. In addition, Randy Johnson was slowly regaining his full strength and command on the mound, and was beginning to look like the same dominating pitcher he had been in 1995. Newcomers Jeff Fassero and Jamie Moyer were also throwing well. Only the bullpen continued to present a problem.

But his skills on the baseball field weren't the only thing that made Junior special. His affinity for the fans and especially the kids was also becoming more noticeable. The Mariners finished the month of April with a three-game series against the Yankees in New York. During the series, Junior had a special guest for one game, an eleven-year-old boy from Harrisburg, Pennsylvania.

It began in spring training when Junior was watching a talk show on television. The boy was a guest on the show along with his mother. The eleven-year-old told the host that Ken Griffey, Jr., was his only male role model. Immediately after the show, Junior called one of his agents and told him the story.

"I want to meet the kid," he said. "Let's make it happen."

So he brought the youngster and his family to New York at his expense and made him a special guest at one of the games. No, the story didn't have a Hollywood ending. Junior didn't hit a home run that night.

But he did hit 11 more home runs in May. That enabled him to break his own record of 22 round-trippers by the end of baseball's second month. He now had 24, and talk about the record continued. In early June the media crush really began. Night after night, reporters wanted to know about home runs and about the record. Teammate Jay Buhner marveled at the way Junior handled himself under the increasing media crush.

"Every day it's the same question," Buhner said. "He does a good job of trying to keep a straight face and give them a nonsarcastic answer. Could I do that? No, no way. I couldn't put up with half the stuff he has to put up with day in, day out. The way he's able to put all of that beside him and still go out and play the game better than anyone else, it takes a special person. That's why guys like him don't come around very often."

But the questions continued. The media crush in

the 1990s is greater than at any other time in history. There are more cable TV stations, more radio sports talk shows, newspapers, and magazines. When Roger Maris broke Babe Ruth's record in 1961, the stress was so great toward the end of the year that his hair actually began to fall out. And the media assault then was nothing like it is today.

One day a reporter asked Junior who the best player in the game was. How many athletes are going to say "I am," without risking being called cocky and arrogant? And how many are going to say "He is," opening themselves up to all kinds of comparisons? Some players, in fact, would refuse to answer, telling the reporter flat out that it was a stupid question. Yet Junior answered the question coolly and confidently, without becoming outwardly irritated.

"I don't even care," he said. "Everybody says it's me and Barry [Bonds]. I can't worry about what Barry does. People have to compare everybody. They ask me, 'Well, who do you compare yourself to?' I compare myself to myself. If there are things I have to work on, I do it. I don't think about who's better, who's worse.

"My dad always says just play and play hard. If [Manager] Lou [Piniella] asks me to bunt, I bunt. My dad always says, 'Be yourself, don't try to be anybody else. You're my son, I'll always love you. Don't worry about what anybody says. People will always try to bring you down.' "

In other words, Junior wasn't going to let the press or anyone else get to him. He knew a lot of media people love to create controversy, get one player to say something negative about another. So he always thought carefully before speaking, kept his answers short and to the point. But he did understand a player's obligations and remained available and courteous. When asked another time if all the media scrutiny was wearing on him, he said, "You have your days where you don't want to answer any questions," he said, "but everybody has a job to do. What bothers me, though, is people sit behind a computer all day, projecting things. Some of those numbers are very unreachable. No matter what a person does, like myself, if I don't hit x amount of home runs, I had a bad year.

"I'm myself, and if people don't like what I do then that's on them. I go out and play hard and give you what I got."

Not surprisingly, Junior's pace began to slow in June. He was still hitting well, but not hitting the ball out as frequently. He would wind up with just five homers in June, giving him 29 for the year. In 1994, he had 32 by the end of June. But at month's end he learned he was once again the top vote-getter among the starters for the American League in the upcoming All-Star Game. This time Junior got 3,514,340 votes, nearly a million more than runner-up Cal Ripken, Jr. That showed his great popularity among the voters.

"I'm not surprised [by the vote]," said former teammate Tino Martinez, himself voted into the starting lineup at first base. "He's the best player in the game and, like I've said before, he relates to the fans and the kids better than anyone."

It marked the eighth straight year Junior had

been named a starter. He was happy for another reason, as well.

"I'm happy because this time I get to play," he said, referring to his injuries the past two seasons. "Maybe I shouldn't say that because I have seven more games left."

But he didn't get hurt. Of more concern than the All-Star Game was that he wasn't hitting the long ball again in July. When the Mariners came to New York to play the Yankees on July 25, Junior hadn't homered in 15 games. He had walloped number 30 back on July 5 and hadn't hit one since. In fact, he had gone some 59 at-bats without a homer, his longest drought of the year. Much of the talk about his breaking the record stopped.

That night, Junior finally tattooed one, getting number 31 off the Yanks' David Wells in an 8–1 Seattle victory. The other high point of the game was that winning pitcher Jamie Moyer raised his record to 11–3. With Randy Johnson closing in on 15 wins and Jeff Fassero also in double figures, the Mariners had three reliable starters. They were still leading the West and seemed a good bet to make the playoffs.

Shortly afterward, two things happened that would create extra excitement for the remainder of the season. The first was that Junior began hitting home runs again. And the second was the surprise trade of Mark McGwire on July 31. The big slugger went from the Oakland A's of the American League to the St. Louis Cardinals of the National League. McGwire had 34 homers at the time of the trade. He and Junior, who had 32 at the end of July, had been running neck-and-neck for the A.L. homer lead. The year before, McGwire belted 52.

Now that McGwire was in the National he would have to adjust. But if he hit enough National League homers to total 62 for the year, it would still be a new record. The trade meant that fans in both leagues would now have something special to watch for the remainder of the season.

Chapter 13

An Epic
Home Run Race

When Junior got hot again in August, talk of the record revived. And after a slow start with the Cardinals, McGwire also began clubbing the ball. So the race was really on, though both players were given only an outside chance of cracking Maris's mark. Junior's mere three homers in July really hurt him, while McGwire's period of adjustment to National League pitching slowed his pace. But their pursuit of the record during late August and September would bring some added excitement to the 1997 season.

The Mariners were continuing their march to the playoffs, though the team was being somewhat derailed by a very shaky bullpen. That gave the California Angels a chance to make a race of it. Because they feared the Angels overtaking them, the Mariners made a trade, giving up a great young outfield prospect in Jose Cruz, Jr., shipping him to Toronto for relievers Mike Timlin and Heathcliff Slocumb. They hoped one of the two could assume the all-important closer role.

As for the team's hitting, it continued to be the best in the league. Though Martinez, Rodriguez, and Buhner all had numbers slightly down from 1996, they were nevertheless having fine years and giving Junior plenty of support. Third sacker Russ Davis, catcher Dan Wilson, first baseman Paul Sorrento, and second sacker Joey Cora were also hitting well, the first three supplying even more power to a team that was on a pace to break the all-time home run record of 257, set by the Orioles just a year earlier. And the Kingdome continued to rock with excitement as big crowds recaptured the Mariner mania of a year earlier.

The race to the playoffs, coupled with Junior's chasing the home run record, made for a hot time in the old town in September. Going into the final month, Junior had picked up the pace. He had an even dozen homers in August to give him 44 for the season. And in the National League, Mark McGwire was also keeping hopes alive.

The 1997 season was also the first for interleague play. Each team had several series with teams from the other league during the regular campaign, something that had never happened before. On September 2, the Mariners were playing their next-to-last interleague game at the Kingdome against the San Diego Padres. In that one, Junior got off to a good September by blasting a pair of homers against the Padres' Joey Hamilton, keying a 9–6 Seattle victory that put the Mariners up by two games over the Angels.

Junior now had 46 homers with 24 games remaining. To hit 16 homers in 24 games (needed to break the record) was not an easy task. But in his last 27 games, Junior had 13 homers and 24 RBIs, as well as a .385 average. If he stayed hot, then maybe . . .

"When Junior is swinging his bat the way he is right now, it makes everyone's job a lot easier," said teammate Alex Rodriguez. "It's a lot of fun for us to watch him, just like it is for you guys."

By this time, Junior put the word out that he didn't want to talk about home runs or the record. If he did, the questions would be repetitive and endless. Always friendly and courteous, he would gladly talk about anything else, no matter how difficult or controversial the question. One night, a reporter asked him what he thought about the overall state of baseball and his answer was quite candid and revealing.

"I'm not happy with it," he said. "We've lost so many fans, and we're losing the kids to the NBA and NFL. We need a commissioner. Not someone who cares about the owners or the players, but about the game and its survival. We're here to play this game and for the people to enjoy it, for them to want to bring family members and want to coach Little League. I mean, how many Little Leaguers quit baseball because of the strike? How many parents said, I'm not going to take my kid to another game?"

When asked what he and the other players could

do, he answered quickly, "There's 600 guys who play this game. Each one has to do a little part for the game to survive. One person may be able to carry the torch for so long, but it takes all of us to do the right thing. Right now the situation is that it's me. But there are other people doing the same thing, keeping the game alive and fun. It's just my turn, I guess. Soon, it'll be a younger guy, maybe one of the young shortstops—Alex Rodriguez, Derek Jeter [of the Yankees], Rey Ordonez [of the Mets]."

So despite the fact that he was a multimillion-dollar-a-year player and the most popular performer in the game, Junior was still concerned about the overall state of his sport and felt the athletes had a duty to contribute in more ways than just going out on the field every day. It was a refreshing attitude in an era when the me-first, me-only attitude has been taken by so many stars.

On the field, the drama continued. On September 4, Junior cracked another pair of homers against the Twins in Minneapolis. Then the next night, he belted number 49 in a 10–6 Mariner victory. That tied his career best of a year earlier and was his sixth home run in the last four games, eighth in his last 11. He now needed 12 in 21 games to break the record.

On Sunday, September 7, Junior blasted his fiftieth home run of the year, a milestone for him. He became just the fifteenth major leaguer overall to reach the 50-homer plateau. He had 18 games left in which to hit 12 homers. McGwire had 48 home runs with 19 games remaining.

Playing his first game in Kansas City after reaching 50, Junior found the Royals pitchers working him carefully, not giving him too much to hit. In fact, his first time up he received a walk on four pitches, none of which was close to the strike zone. Earlier in the season, when he was asked what it would take to break the record, one of the things he mentioned was that the pitchers had to pitch to you, not around you. But again, he understood.

"You know, we do the same to their players as they do to me," he said. "With first base open, the big RBI guy comes up, he's going to first base. Those things happen."

It was just a matter of how often they would happen. Whether it was bad pitches or just a natural cooling off, Junior didn't homer in six straight games after getting number 50. He seemed to be pressing a little in a September 13 game with Toronto, when he went 0-for-4 with three strikeouts. Again, the chance to break the record seemed to be slipping away. The next night the team whipped the Blue Jays again, winning it on a Jay Buhner homer, his 36th. Their magic number for clinching the A.L. West was now eight. That meant any combination of Mariners wins and Angels losses totaling eight would give Seattle the title. On the downside, Junior failed to homer for a seventh straight game.

During the next couple of games, Junior regained his stroke, hitting his 51st and 52nd. McGwire, in the meantime, had moved ahead with 53. He was beginning to get as many questions as Junior, and was even more uneasy facing the press.

"[Breaking the record] is a longshot now," McGwire said. "If I get there, I get there. If I don't, I've still had a pretty good year. So what's to talk about? How much more can you say about hitting a home run? You have to see the ball, hit the ball. It's not easy to do. It's the hardest thing to do in sports."

But even McGwire admitted that the attention focused on his race for the record and his race with Junior was good for the game. Then on Friday night, September 19, McGwire hit his 54th, while Junior connected for his 53rd.

"Did I know Mark had hit one today?" Junior said, after his ninth-inning homer at Oakland. "There were sixteen thousand fans out there telling me that every inning. But I don't think [McGwire] pays much attention to me, and my job is to help us win games, not catch him."

It was the same theme as always with Junior: team first. But nevertheless, the two players obviously had quite a bit of admiration for each other.

"He's an outstanding player," McGwire said of Junior. "I've always admired him while I played in the American League. He's situated in an outstanding lineup and they're in first place and probably going to the playoffs. I'm happy for him and his team."

As for Junior, he had all kinds of admiration for McGwire's ability to hit a baseball.

"I hit them off scoreboards," he said. "Mark hits them over scoreboards."

On Monday, September 22, Junior and the Mariners went up against the Oakland A's at Oakland. He had hit three homers in his last six games, and before the night was over, he had five in seven games. His first was a line shot just inside the right field foul pole. And his second was a mammoth 425-footer to dead center field. That gave Junior 55 homers with five games left. It also put him one up on McGwire. Could he do it?

"I've seen him in a lot of good stretches," said Edgar Martinez. "If he gets in one of those, he could do it. He can hit a bunch of them in a few days. Hopefully, he can get hot."

A's manager Art Howe also thought Junior had a chance. His team was slated to play the Mariners several more times.

"Sixty-one? Yeah, why not?" said Howe. "He's swinging the bat great. Every time he swings the bat, he has a chance. We'll pitch to him as much as we possibly can. No one wants someone to set a record against you, but we're not going to avoid him. We're going to go against him with our best stuff and see what happens. We're not going to make a farce of anything. If we could get a few more lefties, he'd see one every time."

But Junior never worried whether a lefty or righty was pitching. "It doesn't make any difference," he said. "They have to throw the ball over the plate, too. I just have to be more patient."

The next night Junior failed to hit a home run against the Angels. But something more important took place. The Mariners won the game and clinched the American League Western Division title. Junior was the designated hitter that night and was 0-for-3. He was getting tired, but the title celebration revived everyone. The Mariners would be going to the playoffs once again.

Finally, with just three games left with the A's, Junior finally acknowledged he couldn't break the record. And he did it by taking himself out of the lineup for a day of rest before the first game of the series. He still had 55 homers, the same as McGwire. Each player had three games left.

"Do I have a chance to break the record?" Griffey asked, then answered his own question. "I've got six bombs to go and there isn't any way I'm going to break it.

"The fans may not understand it, but that's the way it is. I keep telling everyone the record's not important. What's important is getting the trophy with all the flags on it [the World Series championship trophy]. This is a team game, not a one-man show."

In St. Louis, McGwire just didn't want to talk about the record. He deferred questions to his teammates, saying, "There's other guys here tonight."

So the chase was basically over. But both players kept swinging to the end. Junior hit one more in the remaining two games to finish with 56 home runs. McGwire did a bit better. He hit three in his final three games to finish with 58, tying the all-time record for a right-handed hitter, a record held by two immortals, Jimmie Foxx and Hank Greenberg.

But both Ken Griffey, Jr., and Mark McGwire had thrilled the baseball world in September, giving fans an extra attraction. The home run chase aside, however, Junior had produced his greatest all-around season and had led his team back to the playoffs with a chance to win it all.

Chapter 14

The Playoffs and Beyond

The Seattle Mariners finished the 1997 season with a 90–72 record, the best mark in franchise history. They had pulled away from the Angels in the final weeks of the season to win by six games. In the first round of the playoffs, a best-of-five, they would meet the East winners, the Baltimore Orioles. The other series would be between the Central Division champion Cleveland Indians and the wild card entry New York Yankees.

It had truly been a great season for the M's. As a team, they had broken the Orioles' record of a year earlier by blasting 264 home runs. They also led the league in runs scored and RBIs. And a number of individuals had fine years, as well. Edgar Martinez hit .330, with 28 homers and 108 RBIs. Alex Rodriguez finished at .300, with 23 homers and 84 ribbys. Buhner hit just .243, but blasted 40 home runs and drove home 109. Sorrento had 31 homers and 83 RBIs. Russ Davis slammed 20 homers, while Dan Wilson had 15. Even Joey Cora had 11 homers to go with his .300 average.

On the mound, Randy Johnson was there again, this time finishing at 20–4 with a 2.28 earned run average and 291 strikeouts in just 213 innings. Moyer was 17–5, while Fassero finished at 16–10. Even the bullpen picked it up toward the end.

But it was Ken Griffey, Jr., who continued to grow as one of the greatest superstars of his era. Junior played in 157 games, batted .304, and scored 125 runs, best in the league. He also led the American League with 56 home runs and led the entire major leagues with 147 runs batted in. In addition, he led the league with a .646 slugging percentage, and in total bases with 393.

Think about the year before. That's when he hit 49 home runs and drove home 140 runs in just 140 games. Had he not missed those 20 games with the wrist injury, he probably would have approached or perhaps even surpassed some of the numbers from 1997. That's just how good he had become. And once the 1997 season ended, he was named the American League's Most Valuable Player.

But none of that mattered now. Only the playoffs were important. The first order of business was the Baltimore Orioles. The Orioles had won 98 games during the regular season and, until slumping somewhat the final month, were considered the best team in the American League. With a solid balance of hitting, defense, and pitching, Baltimore was the early favorite to get to the World Series.

The Mariners had Randy Johnson ready for game one. The Big Unit was probably the ultimate mound force over the past three seasons, even with the back injury in 1996. His three-year record of 18–2, 5–0, and 20–4 totaled an amazing 43–6. That's almost a sure winner every time out. But the Orioles were the one team that gave the Big Unit some problems. In his four 1997 starts against the O's, Johnson was 0–2 and the Mariners lost the other two games, as well. In fact, the big lefty had a dismal 3–7 record against the Orioles altogether.

"Tomorrow's a whole new season, actually," Johnson said, on the eve of the first game. "I don't look at this season as being 0–2 against Baltimore just because I was. I've pitched some quality ball games over my lifetime against them."

The other concern, of course, was the Seattle bullpen, which had collectively blown 27 saves over the course of the season. If the Mariners had a dominant setup man and closer, they might well have had the best record in baseball. But none of that mattered when the first game started at the Kingdome, with a packed house of Mariner fans on hand.

Baltimore threw right-hander Mike Mussina, a 15-game winner during the course of the season. It was scoreless for two innings. Then the Orioles broke through for a run in the third. Two innings later, it all came apart. Baltimore raked the Big Unit for four runs in the fifth, driving him from the mound. Then they scored four more off reliever Mike Timlin in the sixth to really break it open. The final was 9–3 and the Mariners were never really in it.

It was a sharp blow for Seattle, having their ace left-hander roughed up and losing big. The M's managed just seven hits, with Junior taking the collar with an 0-for-4 night. Suddenly the Mariners were in a hole. There was one more game in the Kingdome before the series would shift to Baltimore. Seattle went with lefty Jamie Moyer against the Orioles' righty, 16-game winner Scott Erickson. Moyer had a 4–0 record against the Orioles since having left the team several years earlier.

This time the Mariners struck first, getting two runs in the opening frame, Junior driving home one with a solid single. Baltimore got one back in the second, but then Moyer cruised into the fifth, pitching well and with a one-run lead. In the fifth, the Orioles had runners on first and second, two outs, and Roberto Alomar up.

Moyer's first pitch was a ball. But suddenly the lefty indicated something was wrong and Manager Piniella came out. Moyer had strained the flexor muscle in his elbow and had to leave the game. Lefty Paul Spoljaric came in and ran the count full. Then Alomar connected on a high fastball and sent a drive to the deepest part of the ballpark in center.

Junior raced back with those long strides of his, tracking the ball as he ran. He timed his leap at the wall and went high in the air. For a split second it looked as if he had made another of his unbelievable catches. The ball was in his glove, but when he hit the wall hard, it popped out. Alomar stopped at second and two runs scored, giving Baltimore a 3–2 lead.

Later, pitcher Spoljaric would say of Junior, "The guy's only human. I thought he was unbelievable that he got to the ball. I initially thought he had it."

But it wasn't the 3–2 lead that killed the Mariners. It was the bullpen again. Bobby Ayala came in in the seventh and gave up six runs in one and one-third innings. That was more than enough. The Orioles won by a 9–3 count for a second straight day, the Mariners' bullpen giving up nine of the Birds' 14 hits. The huge crowd at the Kingdome gave their team a big ovation at game's end. The feeling was they wouldn't see them again until next year.

So the series returned to Baltimore, where the Mariners hoped to keep their slim hopes alive.

"Our backs are to the wall," said Manager Piniella. "Our job today is to play hard, win, and extend this series. We're not in a good position, but we can improve it daily."

Edgar Martinez reminded everyone that the Mariners had rallied from a 2–0 deficit to beat the Yankees in 1995. They could only hope to do it again. The pitching matchup featured a pair of 16-game-winning lefties, Jeff Fassero for the Mariners and Jimmy Key for the Orioles.

This one belonged to Fassero. The lefty pitched brilliantly, scattering three hits over eight innings. Meanwhile, the Mariners got RBI singles from

Roberto Kelly and Junior, then added two more on back-to-back homers by Buhner and Paul Sorrento in the ninth, giving the team the cushion it needed to close out a 4–2 victory.

Junior's RBI hit came at a time he was just 1-for-9 in the series. Later, in the same inning, he was picked off first by reliever Alan Mills. Replays showed that he got back safely, but the ump's call only further showed the kind of series it had been for him. Still, with the Mariners taking a game, there was hope. Game four would be a replay of the first game, with Randy Johnson facing Mike Mussina.

The Big Unit was more effective this time. Unfortunately, the Mariners still didn't have any luck with Mussina. A homer by Jeff Reboulet and an RBI single off the bat of Cal Ripken gave the Orioles two quick runs in the first. That would later prove to be enough. Seattle got one back in the second on a solo home run by Martinez. Then, in the fifth, the Birds' Geronimo Berroa hit a solo shot to make it 3–1.

Seattle had its last chance in the eighth when Rick Wilkins led off with a walk against reliever Armando Benitez. But the young righty then struck out Cora, got Alex Rodriguez on a ground out, and then retired Junior on a bouncer to Ripken at third. The big hitters just couldn't do it and the game ended with a 3–1 score. The Mariners had just two hits in their final game of the year. They were eliminated in four games.

Johnson had been heroic this time. He went the full eight innings, giving up seven hits and three runs. He also struck out 13 Orioles. For one of the few times all year, he didn't get the support of his hitters. Junior finished his season with another 0-for-4 and was just 2-for-15 in the four games. It was a far cry from the series against the Yanks two years earlier, when he belted five home runs in five games. But these things happen.

In fact, when it ended Orioles manager Davey Johnson said his team had a game plan for dealing with Griffey, something he deemed key to the series.

"Yeah, we did [have a plan]," Johnson admitted. "But I'm not going to talk about it here. We may have to face him again. We just weren't going to let him beat us. It was our pitching coach, Ray Miller, who said, 'If Junior gets involved or gets a big hit, it seems to open the floodgates. He's the point guy.'

"So Ray wanted our guys to walk him, pitch around him, do anything you want but don't let him beat you."

By the sound of it, Junior simply did not get a lot of good pitches to hit. But he wouldn't make excuses.

"You've got to hit when you're supposed to," was all he said.

Later, some of the Mariner players expressed their hope that the team could stay basically intact to try again. That's not always easy in an era when players change teams often, following the big bucks. For instance, some questioned the mid-season trade of young Jose Cruz, Jr., who looked like a coming star, for a couple of relief pitchers, neither of whom was considered a top closer. But for the most part, there were a lot of hugs in the clubhouse, some anger, some tears, yet still optimism for the future.

"We won 90 games for the first time ever in Seattle," Manager Piniella said. "We drew over three million fans [for the first time]. We won our second division title in three years. I told our kids after it was over that they had nothing to be ashamed of. They played their hearts out all year. We fell short in our goal, but when you get to this level of competition, that can happen."

"I'm proud of being a Mariner," said an emotional Jay Buhner. "I remember us finally reaching .500. What's so frustrating is that we had chances to go further, but we haven't done it. . . . It only lasts so long. We've got guys signed for one more year. If we lose a player like Edgar [Martinez], we lose a quiet leader. We can't afford to lose a dominating guy like him. My God."

As for Junior, he was well aware what had happened against the Orioles, but once he was over the initial shock of losing, he preferred to look at the positive.

"Our season's over, we all go home, in different directions," he said. "Then we all think about spring training. You can't say you had a bad season if you don't win the World Series. Houston didn't have a bad season. San Francisco didn't have a bad season. If you go out there and have good years, you see what happens afterward. You can't say that only one team [the World Series winner] has a good season every year."

* * *

Ken Griffey, Jr., is surely a player who has a good season every year. In fact, most of his seasons in the majors have been simply great. Only injuries have slowed him. At the end of the 1997 season he was just twenty-seven years old. Yet in 1998, he will already be a ten-year veteran of the big league wars. And in the eyes of many, he still hasn't reached his peak.

Junior finished the 1997 season with 294 life-time home runs. Not counting the 1995 season, cut short by a serious injury, he has averaged 47.5 home runs over his last four years. And he still missed games during that time due to the strike and lesser injuries. If he keeps up his current pace, he could wind up among the all-time leaders.

In fact, Junior was asked during the 1997 season if he foresaw himself playing 19 seasons, like his father had done.

"A lot has to depend on my physical condition and what my family really needs from me," he said. "Money is not the thing that drives me. I've got all the money. I want to make sure that my family is taken care of. You know, once baseball's over, I've got to stay with them.

"I've got a three-year-old son and a baby daughter at home. After every game, [my son] rides with me back to the house and tells me what he did all day. Then I'll go tuck him into bed or we'll watch SportsCenter. I hope to give him the same values my father gave me."

With the Griffeys, it all goes back to father and son. Theirs is one of the few cases in baseball history where the father was a genuine star and the son became a superstar. In fact, Ken, Sr., is surely aware that his son, before he is done, may be one of the greatest who ever played the game.

"I'm very, very proud of him, so proud you can't put it in words," Ken, Sr., said in 1997. "What I'm very happy about is what he does off the field, how he handles his fame and fortune. I'm a proud dad. And, yes, he'd a good dad, too. He probably doesn't discipline his kids as much as I disciplined him."

Junior—who has the respect of the entire athletic world for his great talent, bright smile, and fan-friendly demeanor—fully knows that he is the result of the strength and love that came from his parents. And he is grateful to both of them.

"My dad didn't care if we watched him play," Junior has said. "He cared about spending quality time with us. We did things or we just wrestled with him. And he wasn't like one of these guys who don't play with other kids. He was out there with all the kids in the neighborhood playing football, basketball.

"I mean, he was Dad. He was cool. I owe him so much. I love him so much."

Junior listened and learned, overcame some early adversity, became a star at nineteen, a superstar soon after. It's almost like a fairy tale, but then again, you need a special kind of man to make it happen that way.

About the Author

Bill Gutman has been a free-lance writer for more than twenty years. In that time he has written over 150 books for children and adults, many of which are about sports. He has written profiles and biographies of many sports stars from both past and present, as well as writing about all the major sports, and some lesser ones as well. Aside from biographies, his sports books include histories, "how-to" instructionals, and sports fiction. He is the author of Archway's *Sports Illustrated* series, biographies of Bo Jackson, Michael Jordan, Shaquille O'Neal, Grant Hill, Tiger Woods, and Ken Griffey, Jr., as well as *NBA High-Flyers*, profiles of top NBA stars. All are available from Archway Paperbacks. Mr. Gutman currently lives in Dover Plains, New York, with his wife and family.